Robert Brewin

Memoirs of Mrs. Rebecca Wakefield : missionary in East Africa

Robert Brewin

Memoirs of Mrs. Rebecca Wakefield : missionary in East Africa

ISBN/EAN: 9783741345218

Manufactured in Europe, USA, Canada, Australia, Japa

Cover: Foto ©ninafisch / pixelio.de

Manufactured and distributed by brebook publishing software (www.brebook.com)

Robert Brewin

Memoirs of Mrs. Rebecca Wakefield : missionary in East Africa

MEMOIRS

OF

MRS. REBECCA WAKEFIELD,

Missionary in East Africa.

BY

ROBERT BREWIN,

AUTHOR OF "THE MARTYRS OF GOLBANTI," "GOSPEL SERMONS FOR CHILDREN," "SANCTIFIED HUMOUR," ETC.

A MISSION HOUSE, EAST AFRICA.

THIRD EDITION.

London:
ANDREW CROMBIE, 119, SALISBURY SQUARE,
FLEET STREET, E.C.

1888.

Preface.

MISSIONARY work in Eastern and Central Africa has of late years come to hold a prominent place in the attention and sympathy of the Christian public of the world. The explorations of Mr. Stanley, the founding of Missions on the Upper Congo, and in Uganda, as well as the murder of the good Bishop Hannington; and of Mr. and Mrs. Houghton of the United Methodist Free Churches Mission, have all, no doubt, tended to produce this result. It is therefore hoped that the publication of a third and cheaper edition of the story of the life of a brave woman, quietly working, and patiently suffering and dying upon a pioneer Mission Station near the East Coast, for the good of her heathen sisters and their children, will not be unwelcome to those who are interested in the spread of the Redeemer's kingdom in the Dark Continent.

In the final chapter of the present edition of this work many additional particulars will be found which it is hoped will be of interest; and some notes have also been added concerning the state of the Mission at the present time.

R. BREWIN.

BIRSTAL, NEAR LEEDS,
   Sept. 1st, 1888.

Contents.

CHAPTER.	PAGE.
I.—BIRTHPLACE AND PARENTAGE	1
II.—LIFE AT MOUNTSORREL	7
III.—BIRMINGHAM AND EXETER	19
IV.—LONDON AND LOUTH	29
V.—THE VOYAGE	37
VI.—THE VOYAGE (CONCLUDED)	54
VII.—ZANZIBAR AND ITS PEOPLE	72
VIII.—LIGHTS AND SHADOWS	87
IX.—REMOVAL TO RIBÉ	111
X.—DAILY LIFE AND WORK	127
XI.—WILDERNESS EXPERIENCES	149
XII.—WANIKA MANNERS AND CUSTOMS	163
XIII.—VISITS AND VISITORS	186
XIV.—ILLNESS AND DEATH	203
XV.—NATIVES' LETTERS—CONCLUSION	222

List of Illustrations.

	PAGE.
Portrait of Mrs. Wakefield	*Frontispiece.*
A Mission House, East Africa	*Title Page.*
Christ Church, Mountsorrel	3
Market Place, Mountsorrel	8
Old British Consulate, Zanzibar	75
Slaves rescued by a British Cruiser	91
Slave Market, Zanzibar	98
Mahommedan at Prayer	106
Arab Dhows	112
View in Mombasa, East Africa	115
Cheetham Hill and the Mission House, Ribé	121
Portrait of Rev. J. Rebmann	124
Grave of Mrs. Krapf and Child, Mombasa	125
Heathen Wanika of Ribé	133
Mombasa Slaves making mats	146
Slave brought to Mombasa	153
Native Christians of Ribé	167
Plan of Mombasa and Neighbourhood	170
Map of Eastern Africa	171
An East African Village	191
Graves of Missionaries at Ribé	219

MEMOIRS

OF

REBECCA WAKEFIELD.

CHAPTER 1.

Birthplace and Parentage.

MOUNTSORREL, an old and romantic little town in Leicestershire, on the main highway between London and the north-west of England, was the place of Mrs. Wakefield's birth, and the home of her early years.

Its long, wide, clean street of varying granite and brick houses is bounded on the western side by rugged overhanging hills, on one of which a strong castle, belonging to the Earls of Leicester, once stood; but where now, on the hot summer days, sleek red and white cattle hold undisturbed possession, as they look dreamily down upon the thatched and slated roofs and luxuriant gardens below; or rosy-faced children while away the long Saturday afternoons in stringing buttercups and daisies, alike ignorant and careless that the ancient fortress which once proudly overlooked the town was built soon after the Conquest to protect the surrounding country from the troublesome Danes; and razed to the ground by Henry III., in the year 1217, for the rebellion of its owners against that king.

Beyond the orchards and gardens which skirt the opposite and eastern side of the long, quiet street lie rich and fertile meadows, with their tempting footpaths, shady lanes, quaint old stiles, and high, bushy hedge-rows, where great elms and pale, drooping willows look down upon the gentle Soar, that, like a silver serpent, winds its onward way among the water lilies and forget-me-nots, to lose itself a few miles below in the wider Trent; looking, under bright summer skies, as innocent of the wild, desolating floods it sometimes brings, as the pretty little town itself commonly does of ever having had a market held there. Its population is scarcely two thousand souls.

On a fine spring day near the end of March, in the year 1825, a stage-coach might have been seen drawn up before the door of Mr. Richard Wale, baker, of this town, not far from where Christ Church now stands, where it had stopped to take up two passengers. A large number of people stood gathered at the spot; for on this day Mountsorrel was for the first time to send forth one of her daughters, as the wife of a Christian Missionary, to labour, and as it proved, to die in a foreign land.

When, therefore, the Rev. William Fidler led forth his young and beautiful bride, dressed in the plain, neat Methodistic fashion of those days, followed to the coach door by her father and mother, her sister Rebecca, and other members of the family, the greatest interest was manifested by the crowd around; and a stranger, looking down upon the tearful scene from the top of the coach, would have rightly guessed that a loving family was about to suffer the loss of one of its choicest members, and the little community one of its most valued citizens. The last hand-shakings were soon over, and the last words of parting soon spoken. "Good-bye, William, take good care of Anna," was Mrs. Wale's adieu to her son-in-law, while her husband added sorrowfully, and with deep emotion (and, as events proved, with true foresight), "I shall never see you more," and the coach rolled away on the white, hard road in the direction of Leicester, and was soon lost to sight.

As the sister of the newly-departed bride, whom I have mentioned as Rebecca, is soon to become known to the reader as the mother of Mrs. Wakefield, he may, if he pleases, learn something of her inward life by glancing at a page of her

CHRIST CHURCH, MOUNTSORREL.

diary of that time, which is now before him. Miss Wale was at this time twenty-three years of age.

"April 11th, 1825.—I feel that if I am to go forward in the Divine life I must take up every cross. I have been thinking much as to whether it is my duty to take Anna's place in conducting our family prayers. I know I have not the abilities of my dear sister; but that the family worship should be given up on that account I am unable to decide. O for grace to take up every cross. If I am to take dear Anna's place I must have more religion. Do Thou, O Lord, stir me up to seek it. Dear Mr. Brewin did indeed lay a heavy burden upon me yesterday, or rather I brought it upon myself, for not speaking in the lovefeast. Lord forgive me, and let me feel that Thou dost so to-night. I ought to praise Thee while Thou lendest me breath ; for, while I have not so much spiritual joy as some have, nor feel so clear an evidence of my acceptance in Christ as I could wish, yet, such has been the power of the Divine grace upon my heart that, many times I have been constrained to say with Charles Wesley,

> " Ah, why did I so late Thee know,
> Thee, lovelier than the sons of men ;
> Ah, why did I no sooner go,
> To Thee, the only ease in pain ;
> Ashamed I sigh, and inly mourn
> That I so late to Thee did turn."

"Tuesday, August 1st.—I have to-night felt it to be a great cross to conduct the family worship. Thou, O Lord, knowest best why I cannot express my desires to Thee in the presence of others so well as when alone. It seems to go so much against my feelings to make others acquainted with my inward experiences. Perhaps one reason why I felt it so difficult to pray to-night was because I have not at all times manifested such holy tempers as I ought to have done. Be pleased, Lord, to forgive me in this respect through the Son of Thy Love. I would not regard iniquity in my heart. I felt it profitable to-night to read Mr. Entwistle's 'Essay on Secret Prayer.'"

"Sunday, October 30th.—I am thankful I have not a burdened conscience on account of not having spoken at the lovefeast this afternoon. Praise the Lord, I was enabled to break through the snare of the enemy. O that I may have courage to take up my cross daily. I am mistrustful

BIRTHPLACE AND PARENTAGE.

of myself, for my heart is very treacherous. Mr. Doncaster has been preaching to-night from ' Wherefore, laying aside all malice and all guile, and hypocrisies, and envies, and all evil speakings, as new-born babes desire the sincere milk of the word, that ye may grow thereby.' "

Meanwhile tidings of the safe arrival in the West Indies of Mr. and Mrs. Fidler had been received at Mountsorrel; and, during the years that followed, the frequent correspondence carried on between the two sisters deeply inwrought into the soul of Rebecca that interest in and sympathy with missionary work in foreign lands, which deepened and strengthened with advancing years and under altered conditions, and was inherited by her devoted daughter, who now sleeps under the waving grass and fragrant flowers of an East African wilderness.

Miss Rebecca Wale was for many years a teacher in the Wesleyan Sunday-school, conducted a writing class on Monday evenings, held children's meetings, collected subscriptions for the Missionary and Bible Societies, assisted at Dorcas meetings, and was an active member of the little Methodist Society to which she belonged. One of its leading officers, who stood very high in her esteem for his sterling Christian character, Mr. Brewin, she has already mentioned. In the year 1836 he offered her his hand in marriage. She accepted his proposal, and they were married on the 24th of May, 1837. In the course of years God blessed their union with four children, Simeon, Iliffe, Robert and Rebecca, the youngest of whom is the subject and the third the author of this volume.

Her father, Mr. Simeon Brewin, was a tall, erect, broad-shouldered, gentlemanly man, and of a frank and open countenance. He had a lively, cheerful disposition, as keen an enjoyment of innocent humour as had any of his acquaintance for miles round. In business he was a hosier and draper. He was a class-leader and local-preacher, a trustee of most of the Methodist Chapels in the neighbourhood, and several times filled the office of circuit steward. His home was sanctified by exalted piety, and was the abiding place of the tenderest affections and unbroken peace.

Of this family Simeon, the eldest son, died in infancy. Iliffe, an exceedingly intelligent and promising youth, wise beyond his years, and a close student, lived to the age of seventeen, and then died of consumption. Rebecca, the youngest child and only daughter, was born on the 19th of August, 1844.

CHAPTER II.

Life at Mountsorrel.

THE first twenty years of Mrs. Wakefield's life were spent at Mountsorrel, and in its immediate neighbourhood. As a child she was physically strong, and healthy, and had a full, fresh, ruddy countenance. In temperament she was nervous, timid, shy, and easily moved to either laughter or tears. Her childhood was an exceedingly happy one, and was perhaps the most sunny period of her life.

The house itself in which her early years were spent was a comfortable, old-fashioned dwelling in the Market Place, a little to the left of the dome-covered structure shown in the engraving, which occupies the site of an ancient stone cross. Behind the house was a large orchard-garden, and beyond this a pleasant field stretching back toward the high, rocky front of Broad Hill, which closed the view in that direction. The garden was one of those crowded, luxuriant retreats where fruits and flowers seem to spring up spontaneously in disorderly and inexhaustible abundance. In its ivy-covered walls the song-birds made their nests without danger or fear; and here, carefully tending her own little flower plot, or cheerfully helping her mother to gather the ripe summer fruit, or racing merrily around its shady paths, many happy hours of my sister's childhood passed away. The writer calls to mind her rosy upturned face peeping out of her white sun-bonnet, as standing on tip-toe among the tall raspberry-canes, she stretched up her little juice-bestained fingers to gather the topmost fruit; and, in the apple gathering time, looking earnestly up at her brothers among the

leafy boughs and telling them where hidden russet and golden
treasures might be found. Busily engaged at school during
most of the week, she often passed her Saturday afternoons
in the spring and summer time in pleasant rambles over the
hills and through the woods in quest of wild flowers, or in
wanderings by the quiet river in company with her brothers

MARKET PLACE, MOUNTSORREL, (FROM THE CASTLE HILL.)

on their fishing excursions; and in autumn roaming along
the lanes, with bright tin and hooked stick in hand, in search
of the ripe blackberries. Few persons have had a happier childhood than that my sister enjoyed, and she was usually full
of merriment. One day she came home laughing heartily
over an adventure that might have ended in a more serious

manner. She had been for a drive with Dorothy and John Mitchil, children of our nearest neighbours, on a bread-delivering expedition to some of the adjoining villages—for our neighbours were bakers. The last loaves had been delivered, and the main street of Mountsorrel was again reached. The two girls, who sat on the straw, were comfortably leaning against the back of the cart, and John, who was driving, was telling them an amusing story. Suddenly, from its having been insecurely fastened, the part against which they were resting flew open, and in another moment Rebecca and her companion were seated in mute astonishment upon the road, unhurt. Owing to the rattling noise made by the vehicle John did not at first miss them, and from their seat on the ground they could see that, with his face half turned round as before, he was still going on zealously with his story, until, not receiving any encouragement or response, he looked quite round, and, amid uncontrollable laughter, stopped the horse, and waited for his lost passengers, one of whom still sat astonished in the road, while the other was now running in breathless haste towards the conveyance. The recollection of these merry youthful days made bright many a dark and solitary hour in after years in her far-off African home.

The cheerful, pure and attractive form of religion which was daily before her eyes in the life and conversation of her godly parents, exerted a powerful influence upon her mind, and her religious choice was early made. In a letter written several years afterwards, she thus refers to the event:

"The time of my decision for Christ was on October 27th, 1857, the year in which dear Iliffe and my father died. I had for a long time previously felt the powerful strivings of the Holy Spirit of God, and I was not ignorant of the way of salvation; but I did not yield until this night. After hearing a sermon from the Rev. J. W. Ackrill, from the text 'My son, give me thine heart,' I went forward in the prayer-meeting as a seeker of salvation, kneeled as a penitent at the foot of the cross, and was at once made happy by believing on Jesus." To which she adds, "Blessed forever be His glorious name. Oh, may I ever live to His glory. Amen and amen."*

Her brother Iliffe's death, which took place on the 1st day of March in that year, was the first dark shadow that fell across the hitherto bright pathway of her life. It was on a Sabbath evening, about seven o'clock, that she stood beside his dying pillow and watched the peaceful breathing out of his soul to God. "I wish I was with Jesus," were almost his last words. Her father, in reviewing his own life for the year ending June 17th, wrote of this event, "We have had to sustain the loss of our eldest boy. We hoped he would have been spared to us, as he was a great comfort. He loved the means of grace, and the people of God, and we looked forward to his being a useful member of the Society; but he was soon called away. But we hope to meet him above."

How soon that meeting was to take place was not foreseen by the fond father who wrote the above lines, but, while the first snows of the next winter were falling, he himself lay stretched upon the bed of death, and the dark shadow of bereavement again saddened that happy home. On the last evening of his life, as the sorrowing but now narrowed family circle gathered around him he assured them of his perfect peace in Christ. When we asked him, "Is Christ precious?" he answered, "Yes, *very* precious, *very* precious. Praise the Lord. Glory and thanks be unto His holy name." On another occasion, he began to repeat the lines

> "Thee will I love, my strength, my tower,
> Thee will I love, my joy—"

Here his strength failed, but after recovering himself a little,

---

* See "Sanctified Humour," a Life of the Rev. J. W. Ackrill. Jarrold and Sons. Price 6d.

he conversed cheerfully of the better land to those who were present. He died on Wednesday morning, December 2nd, and was interred beside his sons Iliffe and Simeon in the burial ground attached to the Wesleyan Chapel. This double bereavement was, it may be imagined, a severe trial to my sister, now only in the fourteenth year of her age.

Her education, which had been commenced at Mountsorrel, was continued at the neighbouring town of Loughborough, under the care of Miss Charnock; and when, in the spring of 1861, a young ladies' school, formerly taught by a cousin in Mountsorrel, became vacant, Rebecca took charge of it, and continued to discharge her duties as mistress of this school for three years. On the Sabbaths she taught a class in the Free Methodist Sunday-school, and engaged in tract distribution. From a child she was a diligent collector for the Mission funds; and the salvation of the heathen was at all times very near her heart.

Of her life and opinions during this period, some glimpses may be caught in the few following extracts from letters written chiefly to her brother from time to time.

"April 25th, 1861.— I have been to hear Mrs. Phœbe Palmer, at Loughborough. At the first service we attended, the resident minister opened the service: then Dr. Palmer ascended the pulpit, and read a few verses in the 13th chapter in Luke, commenting a little as he read. Then Mrs. Palmer arose and addressed the people. She began:— 'What a privilege it is to pray! And we may all pray,' &c. She spoke chiefly on the gift of the Holy Spirit, urging all to seek for a richer baptism of the same. She spoke for half-an-hour, and then her husband earnestly invited seeking sinners to come to Christ. Fifteen persons went forward. I went to hear them again on the following Sunday evening. The chapel was crowded. Upwards of two hundred persons have professed to receive good during the last fortnight."

"June 10th, 1861.—There were very few persons at the Sunday morning prayer meeting. Mr. Merrick, of Leicester, preached in the afternoon. In the evening, Mr. Start, of Quorndon, preached. He would have held an open air service against the cross, at five o'clock, but the weather proved unfavourable. I have been asked to become the collector for the Bible Society in Mountsorrel, and have consented. It appears to have been neglected lately."

It was in November of the year 1862 that Miss Brewin was called to follow her best earthly friend, her dear mother, to the grave. Mrs. Brewin had spent a few weeks with the writer in Lancashire during the early autumn, and soon after her return to Mountsorrel it became evident that she was fast descending that last slope of the hill of life which brings the weary pilgrim to the river that separates the wilderness from heaven. It was her daughter's joy to smooth this latest stage of her life's journey with overflowing filial love, and, like Elisha with Elijah, to converse with her " till they came to Jordan." A short time before dear mother died, she said to my sister, " Go to the piano and play—

> 'Lift your eyes of faith and see
>   Saints and angels joined in one ;
> What a countless company
>   Stand before yon dazzling throne.' "

My sister accordingly played the tune, but could not sing. Soon afterwards her mother looked upward, and said, " Is that the chariot come for me ? " and in a few moments " fell asleep." This great trial fell very heavily upon my sister's heart. The school at Mountsorrel was continued for a year and a half after her mother's death, during which time she resided with an aunt, in whom she found a mother's watchful care and tender affection ; and so the bright sunshine gradually came back again across the darkened pathway of her young and chequered life.

Two or three extracts from letters, written during the year following her mother's death, may now be given.

"April 22nd, 1863.—Last Wednesday night, at the

Society meeting, we were all brought to account about our attendance at the Class-meeting. Each name on the books was read over, and the number of 'absent' marks given, and the cause of absence was inquired into. We are to have the same thing done every quarter!"

"May 26th.—Yesterday was a great day in Mountsorrel. It was the Temperance Gala and Fete. More than a thousand people came from Leicester. It was a very pretty sight from the top of Castle Hill to see the crowds of people thronging the various roads and paths from Sileby Station. There were three continuous streams of passengers, namely, along the fields by the mill, along the lane, and by the river side, all coming toward Mountsorrel, and in the afternoon thousands of people were enjoying themselves on the hills. Tea was provided in Mr. C——'s yard, granary, &c., and after tea there were many merry games in the large homestead. I presided at one of the tea-tables."

"Sept. 11th, 1863.—Our good West Indian cousins, Mr. and Mrs. Heath and Mr. and Mrs. Cleaver, are still in Mountsorrel. Mr. Cleaver has been trying to persuade me to go back with them to the West Indies on their return. He says how happy they should be to take me with them, and he is quite sure that I should never want to come back to live in England again, with a great deal more to the same effect. He asked me if I had written to you about it. He is so kind. I shall miss them all very much when they are gone, as we have had a good deal of their company lately."

About this time another missionary-elect, the pure stream of whose life was to flow for a time, side by side with that of the subject of this memoir, though destined never actually to unite with it, was preparing to leave Mountsorrel under the auspices of the Wesleyan Missionary Society, for the Island of Ceylon. This was the Rev. John Mitchil, a friend of Rebecca's early years, whose name has already been introduced to the reader. He was now a young man in his twenty-fifth year, possessed of extraordinary sanctity of character;

a considerable scholar, and burning with zeal for the salvation of souls. One of his fellow students at Didsbury college says of him " We scarcely knew which to admire most in him, the actual superiority of his attainments, or his seeming unconsciousness of it. He was a rare and noble character. Though the last man to assume such a position, or to regard himself as holding it, he was felt to be an example to all his brethren." Although the governor of the college had pleaded hard for his remaining there as assistant classical tutor, he received and accepted an appointment from the Conference as Principal of the Educational Department, Jaffna. The pleasant summer of 1863 was Mr. Mitchil's last in England, and after leaving college he spent a few weeks among his old friends at Mountsorrel, where he found in the shade of the woods which flanked his native hills or on the green banks of its winding river, a seclusion which was exactly to his taste. Once during a boating excursion down the river, when Miss Brewin was of the party, some forget-me-nots were gathered, and he came near to uttering thoughts of which none but himself had the remotest idea; which thoughts, however, were not then uttered: and, after repeated delays, the vessel in which he was to proceed to Ceylon finally left England in November.

In one of the following extracts reference is made to his departure

" November 17th.—We have had a glorious week of special services, and several have been converted to God. On Wednesday evening I went to hear John Mitchil, perhaps for the last time. The vessel is to sail again immediately."

" Last night I went to the Wesleyan Missionary meeting. I was painfully reminded that on the corresponding night a year ago our beloved mother was there. It was the last time she was out of doors. How well I remember walking up the street with her. It was a very cold, foggy night, and it was with difficulty that she could get along. But we know that though absent from the body she is present with the Lord.

O may we follow her, looking unto Jesus who is the author and finisher of our faith. Amen and Amen."

"March 16th, 1864.—On Sunday morning, as I was without tract covers for my district work, I went round the hills with some tracts and handbills, which I gave to strollers. I returned by the new road, and called upon a person who has not been to chapel lately. The congregations in the afternoon and evening were rather small."

With the summer of 1864 closed my sister's residence at Mountsorrel. A lady in Birmingham, Mrs. Pinches, a cousin of her mother's, and in delicate health, strongly desired Rebecca's companionship, and thought they might be a mutual comfort to each other if she chose to accept her offer of a home. My sister decided to remove to Birmingham, and after Midsummer the school was transferred to other hands. She thus communicated to me at the time an account of the last day of her school life.

"In the morning after distributing the usual rewards to the little ones, I gave each of my girls a book as a parting gift. In the afternoon they brought a great abundance of flowers, and the usual making of garlands commenced. Shortly before five o'clock they sat down to tea, and when I went into school to see if all was right one of the elder scholars rose, and, uncovering a pretty inkstand decorated with a profusion of flowers, presented me with it in the name of the school. I was quite taken by surprise, but thanked them for their kind gift, and then alluded briefly to my approaching departure. The tears which followed were soon dried up by the sunshine and fun which immediately succeeded the speechifying. After tea we had the usual ramble over Hawcliffe hill, and back again to the school-room. The customary recitations over, a few more games and a tune or two on the piano brought the time for separation, and we dispersed about ten o'clock."

The next few days were spent in preparations for the removal to Birmingham.

Miss Brewin was at this time twenty years of age. She was above the average height, well formed, and inclining to stoutness. Her complexion was between dark and fair, her hair and eyes were of dark brown, and her full rosy countenance was soon kindled to mirthful smiles or suffused with copious flowing tears, as the bright sunshine or dark shadows of life fell upon it.

One morning, a few days after the closing of her school life, an event occurred which for a time changed the current of her thoughts in reference to her own future; and promised also to change the whole course of her life. It was the receipt of a foreign letter, which came to hand just as she was leaving her aunt's with a party of friends to spend a day in Bradgate park. Thither we will now follow her.

Bradgate park, with its wide rolling plains of fine lawn-like grass, its fern-covered hills, crowned with groves of giant trees of ancient growth; its Elizabethan ruins, gleaming fish-ponds, shady glens, and open glade, where herds of graceful deer bound lightly away at the sound of approaching voices, is a summer retreat known throughout Leicestershire far and wide. It was in the mansion here, the grassy halls of which are now open to the skies, that learned Roger Ascham found the youthful Lady Jane Grey poring over a volume of Plato, while the rest of the family were hunting in the park, and where she told him of the "pinches, nips and bobs," which her stern and imperious parents administered to her, with the best intentions, whenever she had incurred their displeasure, and which had driven her to the company of her gentle tutor Aylmer, and to her books.

But it is rather its scenic beauty and delightful picturesqueness than its historic interest, that every summer draws to it so many thousands of visitors. It was certainly this reason that brought over to Bradgate the merry party from Mountsorrel, five miles distant, on Tuesday morning the 19th of July, 1864. Passing on the way the old mansion called Rothley Temple—the birth-place of Lord Macaulay, and, a mile further on, looking down upon the wood-embosomed village of Thurcaston, where the bold Hugh Latimer was born, their destination was soon reached. The day was exceedingly bright and warm, and, after their long ramble through the park, the cool shade of the great spreading trees was eagerly sought by the tired visitors. A white cloth is being spread upon the soft grass, and well-laden baskets are being handed out of the conveyance in preparation for the coming repast. While this is going on under one tree the reader may see under another, hidden from the rest of the company by its great, friendly trunk, a blooming maiden of twenty summers, holding an open letter in her hand. It is closely written on very thin paper, and the envelope bears a foreign stamp. There is a somewhat troubled, tearful smile, upon the beautiful countenance that is bending over it, for the writer alleges that the few little English flowers, commonly called forget-me-nots, which he received during a certain boating excursion down the river below Mountsorrel, have been carefully preserved and are now in fact present before him, reminding him of one concerning whom it is his greatest desire that she would think of joining him by and by in his missionary work in the East Indies. When lunch was over, she took her brother quietly aside, and as they walked to and fro under the wide-stretching oaks she told him frankly, and as he will not forget, with an anxious face, of the surprise the letter had been to her, and talked of the unexpected prospects in life which seemed to be opening up before her. Mr. Mitchil's offer of marriage was ultimately accepted, and her history during the next two and half years must be read in the light of her expected departure for a missionary life in the Island of Ceylon.

It was during this two and half years' correspondence with Ceylon, and mainly, I believe, through Mr. Mitchil's influence, that my sister was led into the enjoyment of a much higher spiritual life than she had before experienced. She was enabled to consecrate her whole body and soul and spirit without the slightest reserve upon the altar which sanctifieth the gift; and, from this time, more fully than ever before, Jesus Christ was the enthroned sovereign of her heart, and His will became, so far as it was known to her, her only law. I think these observations will be fully justified to the reader by the extracts from her letters given in the following chapter.

CHAPTER III.

Birmingham and Exeter.

MISS BREWIN removed to Birmingham on Friday the 5th of August, 1864. Mrs. Pinches' residence was on Soho Hill, Handsworth, about two miles from the town. Here my sister found a truly happy home. She was received as a beloved daughter and a trusted friend. Exactly thirty years before Mrs. Pinches had written to her mother, then Miss Rebecca Wale, "You do not know how dear you are to me. It was your exemplary conduct, your consistent deportment, and your Christian conversation, that first convinced me that there was a reality in religion, a something which I possessed not, but which, from the happiness it seemed to afford you, I wished to have." And now, around the orphan child of her dear friend, this gentle lady drew the mantle of her motherly love.

As my sister's duties in the house were very light, they left her abundant leisure for reading and self-improvement. She attended the Birmingham School of Art, where she executed some very good drawings. She retained her membership with the United Methodist Free Churches, and attended Branston-street chapel, where she joined a class led by the Rev. B. Stubbs. On her way to and from chapel, assisted by Mrs. Pinches' benevolence, she supplied the cabmen with interesting literature for Sunday reading. In course of time Miss Brewin became thoroughly at home in Birmingham, and gathered round her a circle of highly-valued friends.

There are some natures the workings of whose inner life

have to be gathered almost exclusively from their outward actions. It is with the utmost difficulty that they can communicate, even to very select friends, small portions of their inward religious experiences, which, from other minds, pour forth with the freeness of an overflowing spring on every slight occasion. My sister's nature was one of these. She never, except during her voyage to East Africa, kept any journal at all, private or otherwise, and except to very dear friends indeed, rarely unbosomed her religious life, even in her letters. I will now, however, supply some few extracts from her letters to Mr. Mitchil in Ceylon, written chiefly during her residence in Birmingham, referring to her religious experience.

"October 22nd, 1864.—I desire that I may be guided aright in all my ways, and this, I believe, will assuredly be the case, since my every concern is given into the hands of one who cannot err.

> 'Jesus, my truth, my way,
>   My sure unerring light;
> On Thee my feeble steps I stay,
>   Which Thou wilt guide aright.'

is the language of my heart."

"December 26th. I feel more than ever my own weakness; but I rejoice to know that 'in the Lord have I righteousness and strength.' That I may be fitted for whatever lies before me is my daily prayer."

"February 9th, 1865.—There have been many accidents lately through the thaw. I often think how much I have to be thankful for that I am preserved from all these dangers.

> 'To all eternity to Thee
>   A grateful song I'll raise.'

On Tuesday night I was asked in coming out of chapel, after a preaching service, if I did not think that Methodism was losing that hearty warmth which formerly characterised it.

We had only heard one response during the whole service. In large towns it does not seem usual to respond audibly. I hope it is not from want of feeling, although to one accustomed to express joy and desire, a degree of formality and lifelessness may be apparent.

"On Monday afternoon the snow was again very deep. I went to my class; but only four of us were present. As the leader did not come, we held a prayer-meeting, and I had with much trembling to lead the singing. This part of my duty I found more easy than another. It was the first time I had audibly engaged in prayer before entire strangers. Lord help me."

"March 2nd, 1865.—To-day the wind has been very high. I well remember how, at such times as these, my dear mother's thoughts used to turn toward those far off upon the sea, and her prayers were silently breathed for their safety. Eight years ago, yesterday, my brother Iliffe exchanged this world of suffering for one where there is no more pain, and where all tears are for ever wiped away. Each year seems to pass more quickly than the last.

> 'I would the precious time redeem,
>   And longer live for this alone;
> To spend and to be spent for them
>   Who have not yet my Saviour known:
> Fully on these my mission prove
> And only breathe to breathe Thy love.'

O that I may be a vessel meet for the Master's use."

"May 28th.—I have to-night had the pleasure of hearing the Rev. William Arthur preach from 'Know ye not that ye are the temple of God,' etc. I am, I trust, profited by the discourse, and am determined that my temple shall be afresh dedicated to God, and kept free from the 'buyers and sellers.' Lord help me."

My sister's removal from Birmingham was now at hand. Mrs. Pinches died a few days after the date of the last

extract. Under the same date my sister wrote of her:—
"On Wednesday night Mrs. Pinches was very much overcome by a feeling of extreme faintness, which she afterwards told us, she thought was the approach of death. Raising both her hands toward heaven, she exclaimed, 'Victory, victory, through the blood of the Lamb. All is well! All is well.'"

Leaving Birmingham on the last day of June, and paying visits to Leicester, Mountsorrel, Chesterfield, Loughborough, Wigan, and other places, she came by the end of December to Exeter, where, for the next year and a half, she resided with the writer. I give a few more jottings from her letters written during the summer and autumn of 1865.

"August 18th.—My twenty-first birthday is to-morrow. I do hope that if I am spared, the coming year will be one of greater devotedness to God and His service; and that I may be made very useful. May the Lord quicken and keep me. Amen."

"September 18th.—The Mission Chapel at Jaffna (Ceylon), seems to be a very nice one. I am glad to know that there are but very few European Missionaries lying interred in the burial ground attached to it. Still, let me say, had there been many more, I do not think it would affect my decision to come out."

"October 19th.—(Wigan).—All the Churches here are complaining of a low state of religious life. O Lord, revive Thy work! I feel the need of continual quickening, or the enemy gains an advantage over me. But I rejoice to know that

'Plenteous grace with Thee is found,
Grace to cover all my sin;
Let the healing streams abound,
Make and keep me pure within.'

This is my prayer. I always feel such a tremulousness come over me while relating my experience at the class meeting. I have never had courage to do it in a public lovefeast, although I always feel these meetings to be times of refreshing; and I enjoy them much."

"November 3rd.—(Wigan).—I have been much profited by reading the memoir of Mrs. Winslow. She was a truly good woman, a chosen vessel, and 'one of a thousand' as a missionary's wife;—a good example to her followers. Sometimes my heart feels a clinging to my native land. May God prepare me for the future, whatever it may be. My lengthened stay among my friends here makes me feel almost as one of them. The thought of being an orphan and homeless ought to be for ever banished. What continued proof I have of the faithfulness of God. May I ever live to His glory."

"November 30th.—Three years ago, last Sabbath, my dear mother was taken from us to be for ever with the Lord. Though I shall never cease to mourn her loss, I cannot wish her back again to this world of sin and suffering; but would strive to follow her as she followed her Saviour, until we meet to part no more."

My sister reached Exeter on the 22nd of December, and soon felt quite at home amongst her new friends. A revival of religion, which commenced under the labours of the Rev. James Caughey, was going on when she arrived in the city, and she joined heartily in the work. In the beginning of the following year, she formed a class of young disciples, whom she met weekly on Friday evenings, for instruction and prayer. She thus speaks of her new sphere of work.

"February 2nd, 1866.—At half-past six this evening, I am to meet a class of children who have recently been converted to God, but who are thought to be too young to meet in the other classes. I must say I do not feel equal to the work, as I have had no previous experience in this line of things. But I would remember the promise, 'If any man lack wisdom, let him ask of God, who giveth to all men liberally and upbraideth not, and it shall be given him,' and,

I trust that, though it is a new movement, we shall have a good meeting. If Jesus be there all will be well. I expect to conduct the class only until some one else can be found to take it."

"February 16th.—I met my class for the first time on the 2nd instant: twelve little girls were present. I spoke to each one separately; asked them questions, and afterwards read a little to them. Although ill-fitted for the work, I felt blessed in it. We met again, with several additions, last Friday evening, and I think one little girl found peace with God at the close of the meeting. To-night I must meet them again; how quickly the weeks come round."

"March 1st.—At my class on Friday evening about twenty girls were present. I feel at a loss to find something to say to each one, as most of them only reply by 'yes' and 'no' to any question I put to them. We should have a prayer-meeting to-morrow evening, but I think we cannot carry one through. I feel I need more wisdom from above; for of myself I can do nothing."

"April 3rd.—I again met my dear children, and we felt that the Lord was with us, although it was in much weakness that I tried to lead them in the way to heaven. I think there never was so feeble an instrument as I am, but I pray that God may bless my humble efforts for His glory."

"April 18th. On Friday, at half-past six, I met my class again, and with greater liberty. I felt much blessed while speaking to a little girl who was seeking the Saviour."

Meanwhile, Miss Brewin had constantly before her the thoughts of her expected departure to India. Writing on June 2nd, she says, "The one thing in relation to this matter that always makes me fear, is the taking upon myself the duties and responsibilities of a Missionary's wife in that land. I feel, sometimes, as if there could not be one with less ability for such a sphere; and I speak with sincerity. The preparations for the journey, and the voyage across the sea, are obstacles which sink into insignificance, when compared to the one I have above referred to. This always seems to rise up before me when I think of the time, now not very distant, when I expect to see the land whence 'spicy breezes' have for some time past been blowing."

On the 20th August, 1865, she left Exeter in company with her brother, and did not return to it again until January. Visits to the English Lake district, Wigan, Loughborough, Mountsorrel, Market Harborough, and Leicester, joined with preparations for her voyage to Ceylon, filled up the greater part of this time. The beginning of November found her at the house of Mr. W. Wale, her uncle, at Leicester. On the 2nd day of this month, she wrote: 'I begin to feel quite uneasy in reference to my leaving England, as the time is passing very swiftly, and I am flying about from place to place. My dear mother's counsel and help would have been valuable at this time, had it pleased God to spare her. People used to tell me she held a blanket between me and the wind. I often wonder how I am to prepare for that long voyage across the deep, deep sea. Sometimes I am encouraged by the thought that it may be a much smaller difficulty when it comes than it now appears. I ought to thank God for the many mercies I have more than others, and expect the fulfilment of the promise, 'as thy days, so shall thy strength be.'"

If ever there was a time in my sister's life when she had need of the support of the above Divine promise, it was immediately at hand. Trouble was in store for her: deep, crushing sorrow that should enter into the soul. At the very time that she was writing the above lines, the fierce and virulent disease known as Asiatic cholera was raging around the mission-house at Jaffna, which was now never to be her home. The Rev. John Mitchil was assiduously devoting himself to relieving the bodily and spiritual necessities of the many natives stricken by the dreadful pestilence, when it seized him in its relentless grasp, and on the 6th of November, he lay down upon his couch in the study of the mission-house to die. Skilled medical aid availed nothing to stay the ravages of the fearful disease, and on the following day he was informed that his end was at hand. He received the intelligence without the least discomposure. Four European gentlemen were in attendance upon him. On being informed that he was beyond hope of recovery, he proceeded with the greatest calmness to give his final directions respecting the affairs of the mission. He then dictated his father's address in full, and proceeded to send his dying messages to his friends, as follows:—" To my relatives generally : tell them that I have found Christ all He has promised to be; I have no fear." "Tell my father I have tried to walk in the way he pointed out to me." "Tell my mother that I have only gone to heaven a little while before her;" and then he began with much emotion, " She is the best woman—" but checked himself. He continued, " Tell my sister she need not be afraid to trust Christ." He then added, "There is one who will feel it more than any other. Tell her God will provide." At half-past six o'clock that evening, he sank peacefully away. His last audible words were " I am going to Jesus." He was interred in the Mission burial-ground adjoining the Chapel, amid the tears of a large concourse of native Christians, to whom he had greatly endeared himself by the holiness of his life and by the zeal and efficiency of his labours on their behalf.

The heavy tidings of this melancholy event reached my sister on Friday morning, December the 14th, as she was standing on the platform of the Leicester Railway Station, about to take the train for Exeter. It had not yet arrived, and she was cheerfully conversing with Miss Mitchil, and Mr. and Mrs. Wale, who had accompanied her to the station, little anticipating the news that would meet them there. The train drew slowly into the station, and a minister, who was charged to break the tidings, stepped out of it on to the platform, and at once recognized Miss Mitchil and my sister. Moving towards Mr. Wale, he called him aside and told the sad intelligence. Let the veil rest upon the events of the next few moments. It is only necessary to add that the journey was at once abandoned, and for the next four weeks my sister remained with the bereaved family at Leicester, to which place they had recently removed.

On the 18th of December she wrote me as follows : " My Dearest Brother : How can I write to you with a heart well nigh broken, and my spirit crushed down to the ground? Truly the hand of God is heavy upon me : were it not for His all-sufficient grace I should sink. More than ever mysterious are the dealings of God with me. O may these most trying dispensations of His providence be blessed and sanctified to my good. Pray for me that I may be able to say from the heart, ' Thy will be done.' Your loving sister, Rebecca."

On the 16th of January, 1867, my sister returned to Exeter, where, excepting visits of considerable length to Launceston and Bournemouth, she remained till the end of the summer, when she removed with the writer to London. A few more jottings from her letters will close this chapter.

"February 15th, 1867.—For the last week I have been suffering much acute sorrow on account of my severe loss. My grief was most painfully renewed by the receipt of one of my own letters, which was returned to me by the last mail, with the word ' Dead ' written upon the envelope. For several days I have scarcely been able to look up. O, how hard these things would be to bear, if, in the midst of our sorrows we had no sympathising friend above, who was once Himself ' the man of sorrows, and acquainted with grief.' Here I find comfort such as no human hand can give. I feel that

   ' One family, we dwell in Him ;
    One Church, above, beneath ;
   Though now divided by the stream—
    The narrow stream of death.'

I often long to cross over it—it seems but a step—and have done with things seen; but I must be—

'Patient, the appointed race to run.'

May my hold on earth be loose, and may my eye be steadily fixed on Jesus. Perhaps one lesson I ought to learn, is to look more constantly and directly to the great fountain head for all I need. As John said in his last letter to me, so say I—'O, for a closer communion with Christ; a constant abiding in Him, that we may bring forth much fruit.'"

"May 2nd, 1867.—I fear sometimes that my sorrow is unfitting me for present duties, and that I too readily allow various perplexities to weigh down my spirits, instead of casting all my care upon God. O, for a more perfect submission to the Divine will, and a contentment to do or suffer for His sake."

"August 6th.—My brother's holidays begin on the 20th instant, when we shall remove from Exeter. How many painful feelings will be revived by this event I can hardly bear to think of. I shall be sorry to leave all my dear friends at Exeter. I have just returned from visiting and trying to comfort a young friend who has recently lost her mother. She died of heart disease, quite suddenly, one evening as they were sitting together at supper. O, that I may live each moment as if it were my last; then welcome, death! welcome, glory!"

"November 1st.—(London.)—My mind has been very much perplexed of late, and Satan's darts have been hurled very thickly around me. But again I can rejoice in a conquering Saviour, who has safely brought me through the conflict with a stronger desire than ever to live to His glory."

"December 26th.—O, what great blessings the Lord has in store for us. He has of late been enlarging my heart, granting me more of His presence, and causing me to rejoice in Him with joy unspeakable."

CHAPTER IV.

London and Louth.

MY sister's removal in the autumn of 1867 to the metropolis, became, after a time, a very pleasant episode in her history, and some of the friendships formed during the year of her residence there were amongst the closest of her life, and were the last to be formally severed when the time of her final departure from England at length came. Her residence was at Plumstead, and she joined the Beresford-street Church, Woolwich, which was under her brother's care.

She devoted herself with great zeal and energy to the interests of the church and Sunday-school, and soon succeeded in forming a class of young converts, whom she met weekly on Tuesday evenings; and, at length, the Society appointed her to the office of a class-leader in the regular way.

On January 15th, 1868, she wrote to an intimate friend, Mrs. Thorpe, of Mountsorrel. "I should like to have a little talk with you about our departed one. He often seems to be so really present with me. But 'are they not all ministering spirits.' I have lately been committing to memory those hymns on the promise of the Holy Spirit, of which our dear friend was so fond, and have found the exercise to be very profitable. Last Sunday we had a sermon on the subject, when those hymns were sung. You cannot think how often my loss is brought to my mind. Frequently, though in submission, I am obliged to give vent to my feelings in tears. But

" Though at times impetuous with emotion,
   And anguish long suppressed;

The swelling heart heaves moaning like the ocean,
  That cannot be at rest.

We will be patient, and assuage the feeling
  We may not wholly stay ;
By silence sanctifying, not concealing
  The grief that must have way."

" I have been much blessed of late," she continues, " in working for Christ. I find there is nothing so blessed as living for others. God does, indeed, abundantly reward me. We are getting on nicely in the circuit. To God be all the praise. My brother is thinking of removing to Louth next year, and if so, I go with him."

The great annual gatherings of the various Missionary Societies in Exeter Hall, in the months of April and May of this year, brought my sister a feast of enjoyment which she keenly relished. She enjoyed a long walk on a bright May morning, and sometimes would tramp the whole distance from Plumstead to Exeter Hall, about nine miles, to attend the meetings. The circuit with which her brother was connected included within it chapels situate in Bermondsey, Rotherhithe, Peckham, Deptford, Woolwich, and Charlton; and Miss Brewin formed many friendships in each of these places, and became more or less acquainted with friends belonging to the various other London circuits. It was with great regret that in the August of 1868 she turned her back upon the stirring life of the metropolis, to find a home in the quiet little market town of Louth, in Lincolnshire.

Here she became again engaged in such Christian work as was open to her, and gathered around her her last Sabbath-school class in England. She was often to be seen kneeling beside the anxious inquirers during the Sabbath evening prayer-meetings, endeavouring to point out to them the way of salvation, and she dealt earnestly and faithfully with some of her newly-found friends who were not yet decidedly religious. One of these, writing after Mrs. Wakefield's decease, says, "When at Louth she often urged me to decide to be a follower of Jesus, and though I did not do as she wanted me then, I often thought of her words, and since I have found the Saviour I have hoped that when she returned to England I might be able to tell her so, but God in infinite love has ordered it otherwise." The Missionary cause was always near her heart, and in Exeter and London, as well as here, she succeeded in obtaining a number of new subscribers to the Society's funds.

In the spring of 1869 she was again in London, on a visit, and remained for about six weeks, during the "May meetings," making her home with Mrs. Randall, of Woolwich. The annual meeting of the United Methodist Free Churches Missions, held in Exeter Hall, was especially interesting, on account of the presence, on the platform, of one of the earliest of our East African Missionaries. Here it was, in fact, that my sister first saw Mr. Wakefield.

In the light of after events, it may be interesting now to read her own account of the enthusiastic gathering, as she described it in a letter written a few days afterwards.

"By half-past six o'clock, the hall was nearly filled to the back; much more so than last year. It looked so nice from the side gallery where I was sitting, and, at length, only a few seats in the body of the hall remained unoccupied, and many persons were in the back gallery. Mr. Gilbert gave out the hymn, and Mr. Boaden prayed. Then came the report, followed by a short speech from Mr. Miller. Mr. Kennedy, of Stepney, followed. And then came the 'great gun,' Mr. Wakefield; and such a continued round of applause as he received, accompanied by the waving of hats and handkerchiefs, I think, I never heard before. It seemed to be many minutes before it was of any use his attempting to speak. I only wonder he was not overcome by this great manifestation of feeling. I shall never forget it. Mr. Wakefield's speech was over an hour long, and very, very interesting."

During the sittings of the Annual Assembly, in Sunderland, in July and August of the same year, my sister listened to several other missionary addresses from Mr. Wakefield, which, though not delivered in the presence of a large audience, proved to be of considerable interest to her. In other words, Mr. Wakefield offered my sister his hand in marriage, and was accepted.

The Rev. Thomas Wakefield was born at Derby on the 23rd of June, 1836, and during his youth learned the trade of a printer. He entered the ministry of the United Methodist Free Churches in the year 1858, and was appointed to labour first in the Bodmin and afterwards in the Helston circuit. In the year 1861, the establishment of a Mission in East Africa having been determined upon, Mr. Wakefield and the Rev. J. Woolner volunteered for this service. Two German Missionaries were also engaged, and under the leadership of Dr. Krapf, this party of East African Missionaries reached Mombasa in safety. Mr. Woolner was compelled almost immediately to return to England through illness. The two Germans, followed soon by Dr. Krapf, also returned home, and Mr. Wakefield was left alone at Ribé, the mission station, to battle with the work. He suffered many hardships, but was, in the beginning of 1863, gladdened by the arrival of a colleague, the Rev. Charles New. The Rev. E. Butterworth followed a few months afterwards; but fell a victim to the climate in a few weeks after his arrival, and Messrs. Wakefield and New bravely toiled on alone, amid many discouragements, much suffering, and but small success. In autumn of 1868, Mr. Wakefield, by invitation of the committee, returned to England on furlough, and in view of his intended return to Africa, he had now prevailed upon the subject of this memoir to promise to accompany him, and share with him the trials and encouragements of a Missionary life among a degraded tribe of East African savages. She did not take this step in haste, and she never repented it. Her life had, as we have seen, been cheerfully laid upon the Missionary altar years before, and now God was pleased to accept the sacrifice. The dying words of her friend, in India, were singularly realised. "Tell her 'God will provide.'" Her marriage took place at Louth, on the 2nd of December, 1869, a bright wintry day.

The interval between her marriage and the end of February following, when she sailed for East Africa, was occupied in preparation for the voyage, and in paying flying farewell visits to her own and Mr. Wakefield's friends, in Chester, Liverpool, Manchester, Sheffield, Leicester, and other places. One Tuesday afternoon, as the light was fading, she stood leaning upon her husband's arm, beside her mother's grave in the picturesque little cemetery at Mountsorrel; letting her tears fall on it for the last time. Gathering a few leaves and blades of grass from the green mound, she turned mournfully away from the spot, with feelings that it would be, perhaps, impossible to describe; and, a day or two afterwards, the woods and hills of her native place had vanished from her sight for ever.

The last fortnight of her life in England was spent in London, at the house of Mrs. Randall, and was a time of incessant bustle and anxiety, many of the preparations for the voyage not being completed until the latest moment, and others having been until this time entirely forgotten. The time ultimately fixed for their departure, was Thursday, February 24th, and a valedictory service was held on Wednesday, the 16th, in Bath Street Chapel, Poplar.

The Missionary party consisted of Mr. and Mrs. Wakefield, the Rev. William Yates, newly appointed to East Africa, and Dado, a Galla boy, ten years of age, whom Mr. Wakefield had rescued from slavery, just before his visit to England. Of the vessel which was chosen for the voyage of the Missionaries to their destination, it is sufficient to say, that it was the "Emily," a sailing vessel of small tonnage, going by way of the Cape of Good Hope; that it was not intended to carry passengers, and consequently possessed only of the most limited, not to say wretched accomodation for them; that she carried, among other merchandise, forty tons of gunpowder; that the crew consisted of eight seamen, and that there were no other passengers than those already named.

On Thursday, February the 24th, a cold, bright day, Mrs. Wakefield passed through the painful ordeal of parting from many of her dearest earthly friends, and from her dear native land, "for Christ's sake and the Gospel's," never to return to it again. Accompanied by the writer, she and her husband bade their friends, Mrs. Randall and Miss Simmons, a distressing farewell at the Woolwich Railway Station, where, but for an accident, her late Sunday-school class would also have been present; and the sad trio proceeded by train to Gravesend, the scene of many a Royal welcome, and of many a sad, though unnoticed, "Good-bye." Here, a solemn little service was held in the upper room of a restaurant, where were gathered the Missionary party, and many London friends who had come down to witness the departure. The Revs. T. Newton, J. Adcock, and J. S. Withington, and T. Cuthbertson, Esq., each gave short and affecting addresses. All then kneeled in prayer, and the Rev. Anthony Gilbert, with great fervency and solemnity, commended the Missionary party to Him who rules the winds and waves, and prayed that they might be preserved and made abundantly useful in the far off land. Shortly after this, most of the friends returned to London, the writer and two or three others remaining to see the end. This soon came; and, by the reader's permission, the remainder of this day's sad history shall be related in Mr. Wakefield's own words. He says—"After spending a little time on the ship (which lay at anchor two miles down the river) we brought our friends ashore. We took a hasty cup of tea in an eating-house, and about six o'clock were again at the pier. Here the last and saddest scene in the long programme had to come—the farewell between my wife and her brother. I dreaded its approach—

> 'When tears are streaming
> From their crystal cell,
> When hands are linked that dread to part,
> And heart is met by throbbing heart,
> Oh! bitter, bitter is the smart,
> Of them that bid farewell.'

Long ago had my wife and her brother been left orphans, the only relics of a loving family. They had faced the world and fought its battles together; their sorrows, sympathies, and sentiments had been one. For some time past they had tabernacled in the same fugitive habitations, travelled from circuit to circuit together, gathering daily around the same hearth, and bending together at the same altar. The warp and woof of their lives were closely interwoven. It seemed cruel to tear them thus asunder, and put seven or eight thousand miles of land and sea between them. But the time of parting came. One long, lingering embrace, as they stood on the steps near the water's edge: a rush of tears; a reluctant unclasping, and the loving brother and gentle sister were separated. I do not wish to witness such a farewell scene again. As our boat proceeded on its way to the vessel my wife sobbed and wept a great deal, and in answer to my efforts to comfort her she said, 'I am not weeping on *my own* account, I am thinking of Robert, he will be so lonely.' Some one has said—

> Oh! when a good ship sails away,
> I seem to hear upon the wind
> Prayers not for travellers on their way,
> But for the sad hearts left behind.'

"It was a little after six o'clock in the evening when we left the pier. Sorrowfully and silently we stole along the river in the fading twilight, and it was dark when we reached the vessel. Gloomily we clambered over her dark side, the sailors drew up the ladder, and we consigned ourselves to our floating prison. On this, our first night at sea, our minds, necessarily disturbed by agitating thoughts about our friends, ourselves, our voyage, and our work, were like the upheaving restless water that lay about us. Short snatches of sleep mingled with our waking sorrowful reflections, and with many a sigh and upward breathing for Divine guidance, protection, and blessing."

CHAPTER V.

The Voyage.

THE voyage commenced on the next day, Friday, February 25th, at a quarter past twelve, and on Thursday, June 2nd, ninety-seven days afterwards, the anchor was safely dropped in the harbour of Zanzibar. Mrs. Wakefield wrote a full and interesting account of this long voyage; and some extracts from these notes and recollections will form the matter of the present and the following chapter.

"About half-past eight o'clock on Friday morning we found that the pilot was on board, and at a quarter-past twelve o'clock, noon, the ship was loosed from her moorings, and we set sail, with very little wind, and not much motion of the vessel. Several fine steamers passed us, bound for New York, Bombay, and elsewhere. At about dusk, red and green signal lights were hung outside the ship, and about half-past seven p.m. the anchor was dropped for the night. I slept little, owing to the tremulous motion of the vessel and the gurgling sound of the water against the sides. During the next day we passed Margate, Broadstairs, and Ramsgate, which were distinctly visible, and looked very pretty in the distance. At twenty minutes past four we anchored in the Downs. I had my first attack of sea-sickness to-day."

"February 27th—(Off Deal)—Our first Sunday at sea. At eleven a.m. we had service on board, all hands being present except two Dutchmen, who, when the captain afterwards asked the reason of their absence, professed to be Roman Catholics. My husband took for his text the 1st verse of the twenty-third Psalm. Before commencing the service he explained to the crew the motive he had in beginning these services, namely, their good and our own. It seemed strange to us, who had for so long a time been accustomed to form part of a large congregation, to join with so small a company at a Sabbath morning's service, in such a lonely spot, under the broad open sky. I say *lonely*, for although I counted from seventy to a hundred ships anchored in sight of us, we were too far off from them to catch any sound of prayer or praise which might possibly have issued from them. We strained our ears, if perchance the Sabbath chimes of Deal might be faintly wafted to us from the shore, and speak to us of the observance of the Lord's day, as they called hundreds of devout worshippers to the sanctuaries there. But we were not left as too small a number to receive a blessing. Our Omnipresent God was with us manifesting His presence, and cheering and comforting our hearts. We sailed again at two p.m.

"During the afternoon the white, chalk cliffs of Dover were before us, stretching away for a long distance. The castle and town too were in full view. We also passed Dungeness and Beachy Head, the latter late in the evening, and this was the last I saw of dear old England."

"March 1st, 2nd, 3rd, 4th, and 5th.—Of the last four days I remember nothing but continued sea-sickness, day and night, and my being carried from my berth to the deck for a few hours each day, and placed in a large wicker chair, propped up with pillows, and wrapped up in rugs, until it was time to be carried down stairs again. All this time I was unable to open my eyes, or take notice of anything. I was not undressed for several days; and for a week I took nothing whatever to eat, and nothing to drink except a little water. The gales were so strong, and I was so ill, that the captain was strongly inclined to put in at Plymouth; but the desire to make a quick passage by taking advantage of a favourable wind, overcame every other feeling, and he passed on, allowing the winds and waves to pitch and toss us at their pleasure. Oh how many times did I wish for half an hour, aye, even for five minutes' relief from the ceaseless 'rock-rock,' 'see-saw,' 'heave and sink' of our restless ship, thinking that even that short interval might bring back life and energy to my exhausted frame. But such valuable medicine was not to be had in a storm on the heaving ocean."

"Sunday, March 5th.—I arose in time for the service at eleven a.m. All the men, by the captain's request, were present. Mr. Wakefield opened the service, and the sermon was preached by Mr. Yates. I was unable to take my appointed part in the service by raising the tunes, not having strength either to stand up or to sing. Whenever about this time I was able to snatch a few minutes' sleep, I was immediately back again in England, surrounded by my kind friends, generally in my early home, with my dear parents and brothers. Then, again, I dreamed of those amongst whom I have more recently been moving in many parts of England, and from whom, in every place, I have received such abundant kindness. How truly have I realized the fulfilling of that gracious promise, 'When thy father and thy mother forsake thee, then the Lord will take thee up.' 'Bless the Lord, O my soul, and forget not all his benefits.'"

"Tuesday, March 7th.—The presence of porpoises round our ship is announced, but I am too weak to stand, so cannot go to the ship's side to look at them. The vessel's bulwarks are much higher than in many vessels, and so, as yet, I have scarcely seen the sea at all; but I am thankful to be able to open my eyes and look about the ship now and then. I see Dado sitting and looking very quiet sometimes, and can easily divine what is the matter."

"Wednesday, March 8th.—To-day a poor little swallow was beaten down by the heavy rain and wind, and sought shelter on our ship. One of the men found it and brought it to us. I wonder where the little wanderer's home is? It looked up so pitifully, all shivering with cold, and almost asked for a place underneath the warm rugs in which I was wrapped. It lay on my knee, drawing in its little neck, and closing its wings quite tightly, and refusing all food from a stranger's hand, until its little life ebbed away. At this time we were opposite to the Straits of Gibraltar, and distant from them about six hundred miles. This is the second visitor of the kind we have had.

"This week I have begun to take a little nourishment. What should I have said a month ago had any one told me that after fourteen days at sea I should still be too weak to hold a cup or spoon, or feed myself. But so it is. I believe everyone in the cabin began to be anxious about my prolonged exhaustion. Some of them had said I should 'give in,' I should 'never hold out,' and so on. I am thankful to say that during the past few days and nights the sickness has somewhat abated, although my stomach still entirely refuses all solid food. I dare not taste it."

"Friday, March 9th.—Another stormy night. No sleep. Heavy seas washing overhead, and everything movable tumbling about and keeping up a constant rattle below stairs. Mr. Wakefield and myself are again prostrated by sickness."

"Sunday, March 13th.—Our third Sabbath at sea. I am thankful to say I am a little better, and enjoy this bright, beautiful morning. It reminds me of some spent in our lovely home at Mountsorrel, where Sunday seemed brighter than any other day. Soon after eleven o'clock we assembled for worship; all were present except the steward and the man at the wheel. The latter, however, is within hearing distance, the pulpit or desk being formed of the 'companion,' or porch over the cabin staircase, on one side of which the preacher stands, the men sitting opposite on the hen coops; I have my chair on the other side of the companion, so that I cannot see the preacher. Dado generally has a stool beside me; and, when he knows the tune, is quite a help. Some of the sailors can sing very well. Mr. Wakefield took for his text, 'And I saw the dead, small and great, stand before God.' He spoke of Resurrection, Judgment, Doom. I felt it to be a profitable time; the subject was appropriate, and the men seemed very attentive.

"During the afternoon our attention was called by the boatswain to a nautilus, which was sailing along over the now calm and smooth water of the sea. As it was near the side of the vessel, the mate threw over a bucket with a rope attached, and succeeded in capturing this beautiful creature for our closer inspection. It was about six inches in length, its body something like the bladder of a fish, and of a bluish colour. Its 'sail' was semicircular, and stretched from end to end of the bladder-like hull, crimped like a lady's lawn frill, and tipped all round with pink. In substance, the fish was semi-transparent, and felt to the touch like india-rubber. As it was being hauled on board we discovered that a number of blue threads, many yards in length, and looking like strings of blue beads, were suspended to it. These threads stung severely the hands of those who lifted them over the bulwarks.

"About six p m. the moon rose, and we sat on deck enjoying a soft gentle breeze; singing some of the old familiar hymns, and talking of the public services at home. We were then nearly due west of Morocco."

"Tuesday, March 15th.—A very fine day. Mr. Wakefield read to me some of the first rules of the Sawahili grammar. In the afternoon the gentlemen got out their fishing tackle, and suspended long lines over the stern of the vessel, baiting their hooks with white rag, according to the experienced advisers on board. The only thing caught was a tallow candle, which led the captain to remark that we were on the Candle Banks! To-day we sighted Palma, one of the Canary Islands."

"Wednesday 16th.—To-day there was another island visible, a little to the south of Palma. Although we were from twenty to thirty miles distant, we could discern their rugged, mountain-like sides covered with grass and rocks, and O, how I longed to roam for a few hours upon them, freed from the narrow boundary in which we were enclosed. The captain smilingly asked me if he should put out a boat and send us ashore, but it was only a joke, and we had to be content with only a refreshing sight of land after the monotony of twenty days of sky and ocean."

"Thursday, March 17th.—We have now been at sea for three weeks. I am still a little better, and am truly grateful to my Heavenly Father. I was able to sit in the cabin for a few minutes before retiring. We have reading and prayer every evening. To-night the captain read, and Mr. Yates prayed. Then before we rose from our knees the captain began in the greatest simplicity to offer up a few words, telling the Lord He knew it was the first time he had thus lifted up his voice in company, praying for wisdom to guide the ship and the men; prayed God to bless the Missionaries he had on board, adding 'although thou knowest Lord I have no sympathy with them in their work.' On rising he told us how uneasy he felt at times in reference to the state of his soul, and Mr. Wakefield gave him good advice, urging him to seek the Lord at once with all his heart."

"Friday, the 18th.—The moonlight in the evening was very beautiful. We sat and enjoyed it until eleven p.m. I always like to sit up as long as I can, to make the nights shorter, I have so many sleepless hours. I have not yet become accustomed to the tramping of feet and the other noises on deck, and the rolling motion of the vessel."

"Saturday, March 19th.—To-day we entered the Tropics, and the heat is now becoming very great. A nice awning, however, protects us from the hot sun. In the evening I was very ill again, and was quickly driven to my berth."

"Sunday, March 20th.—Feeling better, I got up in time for the service. There was a gentle breeze, and the shadow of the awning was very agreeable. Mr. Yates preached on the Prodigal Son. At the close of the service I lent the sailors some magazines a friend had supplied us with before leaving England. They appeared much pleased, and during the afternoon I saw some of them busy reading. There is a small library on board, furnished by the noble Religious Tract Society, for the use of the crew. In the evening, before the moon rose, the phosphorescent light was visible in the foam along the sides of the ship; and I was able, with my husband's assistance, to stand and watch it. It appeared like stars of varied brilliancy, some only twinkling for a moment and then vanishing, and others sailing steadily past, while with every rush of foam a fresh display was presented. It was like looking down upon another firmament, all spangled with bright gems, like the one above us. The opinions concerning the cause of this illumination of the sea are various. I think the generally received opinion is that it is the light emitted by a species of animalculæ, which have the faculty, like glowworms on land, of becoming luminous.

"The moon rose shortly after nine o'clock. I think the rising of the moon at sea is a more beautiful sight even than the same event on land, the light shining across the successive waves making them look like liquid silver. To-night I saw the bright constellation, the Southern Cross, for the first time, and the North Star was still visible,—the representatives of the two hemispheres. During the evening we sang many hymns from the Sunday-school Hymn-book, and afterwards some from the large book. The following are favourites with us:—'When I survey the wondrous Cross,' 'Peace, doubting heart,' 'How do thy mercies close me round,' 'God of my life, through all my days,' 'The God of Abraham praise,' 'For ever here my rest shall be,' and many others, of which we never tire."

"Thursday, March 24th.—Twenty-eighth day at sea.— It seems strange at this date to be complaining of excessive heat, but so it is. The evening was cloudy, thus preventing our usual enjoyment of viewing and admiring the beautiful constellations overhead. The North Star, our old familiar friend, is nearing the horizon, and in a few days will bid us adieu. This indicates progress on our part, and gives the captain much pleasure. Yesterday, however, we only made one hundred miles in twenty-four hours. The patent log is always lifted up out of the water at noon, and then everybody wants to know how many miles we have come since noon of the previous day. The log tells exactly. The captain always gets very restless if toward evening he can perceive no signs of a breeze. I do not encourage him much, for I always tell him I prefer smooth sailing. As yet, I have not strength to walk across the deck alone. The first time I got up from my chair without assistance, I thought to surprise my husband, who was looking over the ship's side; when, having taken a few steps, I suddenly fell, and only saved myself by grasping at the bulwarks. My keeper-ring at once shot off into the sea, for my fingers have become very thin lately. The captain presses me to take a glass of wine now and then, but I have an objection."

"Sunday, March 27th.—Our fifth Sabbath at sea dawned upon us beautiful and bright, like one of our English June days. Mr. Wakefield conducted our morning service. We have, to-night, lost sight of the North Star. It has sunk down below the horizon in the rear of our ship. Shall we ever see it again?"

"Thursday, March 31st.—To-day we crossed the Equator. There had been a good deal of joking for some days previously about 'crossing the line,' and the visit of Father Neptune to the ship. About five o'clock in the evening, the following scene took place in the fore part of the ship:— 'Father Neptune' (who was really one of the sailors, dressed as much 'in character' as the drapery of the forecastle would admit of) made his appearance, attended by his suite. He had on a flowing white skirt, reaching almost to the ground. Above that, he wore an old-fashioned drab overcoat, a hat of the same colour, a mask, and a very, very long beard, looking like shag tobacco, but being in reality picked oakum. A grey or snowy-white beard would, I thought, have become the god of the sea much better. When all the crew were assembled, Father Neptune, amid profound silence, roared out in a loud voice, 'Is there any one here who has not crossed my dominions before?' Out stepped the youngest seaman, and, in a much more subdued tone, replied, 'I have not.' 'Then come with me,' said the monarch of old ocean. Poor boy! he was taken to a little distance and placed on a seat, while his face was bedaubed with tar by Neptune's barber, who held in his hand a rusty old saw, with the back of which he began to perform, in no gentle manner, the operation of shaving; occasionally wiping the saw on a dripping wet pad which lay on the boy's shoulder. When the scraping was over, the youth, by order of the ocean monarch, jumped into a large cask of salt-water close by, and already prepared for the purpose. In this he was plunged overhead three times. He then sprung on to the side of the cask, and, raising a great shout, was liberated. Two other sailors underwent the same operation. All, however, was not yet over, for Father Neptune had at dusk to take his departure from the ship. This he was *said* to do in a flaming tar-barrel, which was put off from us about seven o'clock, and which continued in sight for nearly two hours, and until it appeared like only a red speck of light far away behind us, hidden now and then by the heaving waves; and at length disappeared altogether, and was seen no more."

"April 1st.—We were agreeably surprised, between six and seven o'clock this morning, by the captain calling down the cabin staircase in a quick manner, 'A vessel in sight, homeward bound. All who have letters for England, get them ready, that they may be sent by her.' Mr. Wakefield at once went on deck, when the captain burst into laughter, and said he only wished to let us know what day it was.

"Soon after breakfast the sky grew dark, and a squall came on. This brought a large number of porpoises round the ship. We could see them coming from all sides, bounding like deer above the fern and long grass of a park, and making fifteen or twenty feet at a leap. They came in large troops, and the sea seemed alive with them. The boatswain soon got a harpoon ready, and standing on a chain a few feet below the jib-boom, watched with eagle-eye their passing and repassing underneath him. At length one rose very near the surface, when, with a tremendous stroke, he lodged the harpoon in his prey; and then, amid great excitement, the men commenced hauling the prize on deck. When hoisted about half-way up towards the deck, the porpoise, as it hung in the air, looked as large as a fat pig, and it was feared he would snap the rope, which was only a thin one, and it was suggested that he had better be let down again until he had well tired himself; so down he went again, and, making a desperate rush in the opposite direction to that in which the ship was going, he broke himself loose from the harpoon and escaped. Then all the other porpoises disappeared: and we saw them no more that day.

"The rain of the morning continued throughout the day, and every available vessel was used to catch it; for our water supply was getting low, and we were about to be put upon a daily allowance. After dinner the excitement of catching the water was increased by, first, the mate, and then the passengers, commencing a washing-day. It was amusing to see Mr. Wakefield, seated on a camp-stool, with a bucket before him for a wash-tub, and his sleeves turned up, soaping and rubbing away at the clothes quite scientifically, although he declared it was the first time. Dado adopted an Eastern mode, which was quite new to me. Taking off his shoes and stockings, and holding fast with both hands to a rope above him, he jumped up and down upon the clothes, in this manner expressing many unnecessary adhesions in a novel, and, perhaps, less laborious fashion. At first I could only laugh and look on; but at length, the captain having found me some blue, I finished off my husband's work, and certainly, when the clothes were dried they were a first-rate colour. On that evening we were all well tired, and even the next day the gentlemen complained of fatigue."

"Saturday, April 2nd.—The sea is still very calm, and we are making but little progress. This morning we spoke a Dutch barque, bound from Rotterdam to Batavia. There being little or no breeze, she kept in sight of us all the day, and seemed quite like a neighbour. In the afternoon, about half-past two o'clock, the captain determined to put off a boat on a visit to the Dutchman, the object of which was to purchase some brushes for use on board. The boat was manned by the mate and three sailors; and Mr. Wakefield, Mr. Yates, and Dado, were the privileged passengers. They appeared highly delighted to get away, if only for a few hours, from the narrow boundary line of the 'Emily's' sides. The sea was beautifully smooth, and only moved by those gentle upheavings which are always felt during a calm; and away their little boat was borne towards our friendly neighbour, which lay as if at anchor about three miles distant, just too far away for me to discern the visitors clambering over her side. To me, who was all the time watching, they seemed to be a long time gone, and I began to weary for their return, which took place about five o'clock. They found the captain of the Dutch vessel exceedingly kind and generous, and a lady who was on board sent me some nice delicacies to tempt my flagging appetite. For all these kindnesses they refused to receive any recompense. Soon after the boat returned a sudden and very heavy squall came on, and we were all very thankful that our friends had returned in time to escape a complete drenching."

"April 3rd.—Another beautiful Sabbath morning has dawned upon us. Hitherto we have been much favoured in having fine weather on this day. Mr. Yates preached from a very comforting text, 'I will never leave thee.' The day passed very quietly. I lent the sailors some copies of the *Illustrated Missionary News*, with which they were much pleased. I had too much headache to read more than a few lines at a time. I am getting tired of life on board ship, and am beginning to think that not until my feet are once more planted on *terra firma* will my health be restored to me."

"April 10th.—Our sixth Sabbath at sea. Early this morning the truss-band of the mainyard snapped in two; and in consequence of this accident our little service was postponed until the evening. This, too, was a pleasanter time; for the heat of the morning had somewhat abated, and the moon soon arose in all her tropical splendour, shedding a glorious light over the deck, where we were assembled, and mingling strangely with the light of the two lamps, which were now rendered almost unnecessary. It was a novel scene, but was not unnoticed by the ever-watchful eye of the Lord of Hosts, and, though on the splashing, rolling sea, we received a portion of His special blessing. Mr. Wakefield preached on the 'Rich man and Lazarus.'"

"April 15th.—Good Friday. This was like a midsummer day with us, and we thought much about our friends in England. The sailors had a holiday, put on their best clothes, and enjoyed the day as they thought best. In the evening we sat on deck, and sang several of Wesley's hymns, appropriate to the day."

"Easter Sunday, April 17th.—Our eighth Sabbath at sea. After one of the roughest nights we have yet had, during which I had the greatest difficulty in preventing myself from being pitched unceremoniously out of my berth, I rose to enjoy another glorious Sabbath morning, which presented an almost cloudless sky. The vessel was still tossing considerably, and lay very much on her side. Service at 11-20 a.m., conducted by Mr. Yates. We sang in unison, as we thought, with thousands of our friends in England, the hymn commencing

'Christ the Lord is risen to-day.'

and, with them, rejoiced in a risen Saviour, who has broken

the barriers of the tomb, and taken away the sting of death. Mr. Yates preached from Galatians vi. 14. In the afternoon I thought much about my late Sunday-school class at Louth, and wondered if, since I left England, any more of its members had embraced religion. May God bless them, and save them all."

"At two o'clock p.m. to-day we passed out of the Tropics; and the temperature is becoming much cooler."

"Monday, April 18th.—A fine day. 'A ship ahoy, and fast coming up with us' is the news. A fine vessel she looks at ten miles distance, and yet at her present rate of sailing she will soon be up with us. Right. Here she is alongside, quite close, and making our little 'Emily' look like an untidy 'long boat.' She proves to be the 'Windsor Castle' from London. The two captains are conversing together without the aid of the trumpets. There appear to be about half-a-dozen passengers on board, three of whom are ladies, and one holds a baby in her arms. All are dressed as if for dinner, and, standing on the high poop, look down, perhaps in two senses, on our poor little vessel. They nevertheless appeared to be as much interested in us as we were in them, and, waving handkerchiefs and hats in a friendly manner, bade us good-bye as they passed swiftly on their way. They were bound for India, and ours was the first vessel they had sighted since leaving London. Soon they left us far behind, admiring their stately vessel and the proud way in which she seemed to ride over the water at an amazing speed."

"Wednesday, April 20th.—We have been sailing of late towards the shores of South America; but have at length altered our course, and are now sailing in a south-easterly direction towards the Cape of Good Hope. Some one remarking that the weather is still very warm, the captain replied that we must make the most of these fine days, for that they will soon be all over, as we are approaching the region of storms. About noon to-day two ships came in sight, one apparently crossing from the Cape to La Plata, the other 'homeward bound.' Oh, what a thrill ran through our whole natures at the announcement 'a vessel homeward bound,' and how excited we all got, as if perchance she were going to take messages from us to our friends in England. The English ensign was soon hoisted, and to this salute our captain replied 'Good morning,' by raising and lowering ours three times. The other vessel was going much faster than ourselves, and had no sooner commenced signalling than she was up with us, and near enough to shout to us, 'Where from?' 'Whither bound?' 'What is your longitude?' and so on, and had quite passed us before we could ask our questions, and we only learnt that she was bound for London. They saluted us with the waving of hats and handkerchiefs, and the sailors also gave us a loud 'hurrah.' I don't think our men returned the greeting; their spirits might not have been so buoyant as if their faces had been turned the other way. It always seems to put new life into us to speak with a vessel, and furnishes us with a new theme for conversation for some time afterwards."

"Thursday, April 21st.—Our fifty-sixth day at sea. The day is rather cloudy, with slight showers of rain. This afternoon we spoke a Welsh vessel, bound for Rangoon. The captain, a tall Welshman, brought his vessel close alongside, and our captain and he had quite a friendly conversation together. This barque left London ten days later than we did, and crossed the line on the same day. Both captains complained of want of wind."

"There was a magnificent sunset to day, about half-past five ; the most gorgeous we have yet seen. The whole sky from above our heads down to the horizon was one great mass of glittering gold ; while behind us the reflection was scarcely less beautiful, but different, being of a soft rosy hue."

"Sunday, April 24th.—Our ninth Sunday on the wide, lone ocean. When shall we get to Zanzibar? I sat down to breakfast at the table this morning, for the first time since we put out to sea. It was a beautiful morning, and the sea was as smooth as glass. There was no wind, but the huge swell of the sea is carrying us onward at about one mile an hour.

"At such a time as this there is generally an interesting display of various kinds of small jelly fish, which come gently floating past on the surface of the clear blue water. Some have feelers, like fibrous roots, attached to them, and suspended in the calm water we can see them to perfection.

"We had service as usual at 11.20. Just before Mr. Wakefield gave out his text, the ship gave such a tremendous lurch as threw nearly every one off their seats. One came tumbling from some distance into my lap, and then as quickly, by an opposite motion of the ship, was hurled back again towards his seat, while the men who were sitting on the hencoop suddenly rushed forward in a body towards the pulpit, as if they had urgent business with the preacher. I wondered that both preacher and congregation retained their gravity, but only Dado, who laughed outright, appeared to be tickled by the strange scene. During the sermon there were several interruptions of the same kind, but a few moments' pause soon set all to rights again. My thoughts at such times as these always rush home, and we think of the contrasts our position presents with the ease and comfort of our worshipping assemblies in England.

"This afternoon we spent as usual in reading. The sun set at half-past five o'clock, and we had a long evening on deck, talking and singing in the light of the stars; for we have lost the moon now. When she reappears the captain hopes to have the advantage of her light in steering through the Mozambique Channel, through which he has never passed before. To-night the 'Magellan clouds' have been pointed out to me for the first time. They appeared like two small pieces of white haze. One is situated in the centre of the Milky Way, and forms part of it; the other is a little further south. They are both, not clouds, but groups of stars. I feel thankful to God that I have been much better in health to-day."

"Monday, April 25th.—To-night our great anniversary missionary meeting is being held in Exeter Hall. During the earlier part of the evening we were all sitting on deck in the darkness, till the piercing wind and falling rain drove us below. We heartily wished our friends in London a good meeting, and to crown all, a good collection. Little did I think, twelve months ago to-night, when I first saw Mr. Wakefield, where I should be if spared for another year. 'Thou shalt guide me with thy counsel,' has ever been my motto, and I have full confidence in the wisdom and goodness of that God who has hitherto directed my steps. Oh, that I may be fully fitted for the sphere in which I am expected to move!"

"Tuesday, April 26th.—'Through much distress and pain' is now our experience. We have had a terribly rough night, with little or no sleep, through the heavy lurching of the vessel, which kept us in constant fear of being played with by the storm as were our boxes, books, and trunks; which were being flung from one end of our berth to the other, to and fro, until at last an army of them lay scattered on the floor.

"In the afternoon I sat down to read, but was soon called on deck by the captain to come and look at the sea in her strength, before he commenced taking in sail. With some difficulty I managed to climb the narrow staircase and get to the side of the ship, although both Mr. Yates and the captain lent me their assistance. The sea was dashing over one side of the vessel, which was now and then completely under water, the sea rising from its side like a real hill on land, which only wanted solidity and a green grass covering to make it quite tempting. I felt afraid to stay long on deck lest I should slip and get a bad fall.

"Not that below it is all quiet. At tea-time we had great difficulty in assisting ourselves, and should have lost our plates and their contents a dozen times if we had not held them in one hand. As it was, a few plates, a saltcellar, and the ignited oil lamp, disappeared from the table without notice.

"We had a terrible night. Nothing but shocks at the loud noises, and sudden frights at our narrow escapes from being violently hurled, like our boxes and baggage, from side to side of our narrow enclosure. Then there was the incessant 'drip, drip, drip' of water from above, first on your arm, then on to the end of your nose, and a merry little stream trickling at your feet, wetting everything through before morning. Then the floor was in a most pitiable condition, and all the boxes drenched in water."

CHAPTER VI.

The Voyage (Concluded).

"THURSDAY, April 28th.—Our sixty-third day at sea. At three o'clock this afternoon, we sighted the Island of Tristan d'Acunha, for which we had been steering for some days. The island was ten or twelve miles to the eastward of us, and appeared like a huge mountain, the summit of which, 8,000 feet above the the sea, was hidden by the clouds. We went on deck for an hour after tea, and afterwards, as we sat in the cabin, one of us read, another wrote, and a third engaged in the sublime art of mending stockings."

"Sunday, May 1st.—Our tenth Sabbath at sea. This was a cold bleak day; a keen wind was blowing, and our warmest garments were in full request. At 11.20 a.m., the usual service was held; not, however, on deck, but in the cabin, on account of the cold, and the rolling of the vessel. After tea, we went forward to the ship's bows, to watch the beautiful phosphorescent light, which appeared to be thrown from underneath the ship with the rushing foam. It seemed as though a row of jet lights must be hidden somewhere out of sight, and produced a singular and beautiful effect."

"Tuesday, May 3rd.—To-day we have crossed the meridian of Greenwich, and our course is now due eastward."

"Friday, May 6th.—The last night was a fearfully stormy one. We got no sleep, and, what was worse, such a tossing, shaking, bumping, and drenching, as has quite knocked me up for to-day. The cold, too, in these latitudes is very severe, and all the wrappers and woollens I have at command are scarcely sufficient to keep me from a constant shiver. Exercise might alleviate this; but it is not available on a small vessel; and, besides, the decks are very wet and slippery, and the ship is rolling very heavily. If I go on deck, one of the sailors will say, 'It's not fit for you to be here, mum—you'll be safer down-stairs, mum.' Then I go downstairs, and to my berth, and try to get a little sleep. But all is of no use; my nerves will not get reconciled to this sickly 'see saw, see saw,' of what should be my resting place. Oh, for some solid ground to rest upon; some little spot, so small, so humble, so it be but firm, and free from this incessant motion, which rocks my brain, and distresses my whole system. My husband brings me a dose of quinine, and I feel much better."

"Saturday, May 7th.—Another restless night, from the springing and rolling of our little ship. Apart from this, the noises were enough to make me fancy that our floating abode was being demolished; its planks and beams creaking and groaning with a deafening sound. Every few minutes there was a loud crash against the ship's side, as if we had struck on a coral reef, or, like a drunken man in a narrow lane, were driving against a wall, first on one side and then on the other. Then sudden and entirely unexplainable explosions seemed to be going off with a loud crack, till we could not hear our own voice or that of a near neighbour, without stretching the oral nerves considerably."

"This morning, about eleven o'clock, I joined Mr. Wakefield and Mr. Yates at the top of the cabin stair-case, to watch the sea. I shall never forget what I saw as I stood there. A strong gale of wind was blowing from the southwest, and old ocean in all his pride, grandeur, and magnificence, was rising. The waves rose first to a great height, and then, as they curled over, showing their proud white crests and clear blue transparency beneath, suddenly sank into a deep valley, which stretched for a long distance to the right and left of us. Then immediately before us rose a mountain-like wave, over which it seemed impossible that the 'Emily' could ride; but—bravo!—over she goes with a toss of her head, and down we sweep on the other side, only, as it seemed inevitable, to be swallowed in the jaws of the deep. Then we were amused by a large boiling wave rolling up to the side of the ship and splashing itself on to the decks, hiding from our view for a moment one of the sailors, and, in not a solitary instance, one of the cabin passengers, to the no small diversion of those who escaped the drenching. The decks were, of course, flooded; and, as the water rushed from side to side of the ship, it sometimes threw down the sailors, who, during this squall were very busy in hauling ropes, and altering the sails, at the command of the captain, who, whatever the weather, is always at his post."

Sunday, May 8th.—If, on Friday night, we were tossed to and fro by every wind and tempest, what shall I say of the one we have just spent? Language utterly fails to give to a landsman a true idea of the extreme wretchedness of a stormy night at sea, with not a moment's true repose. Every now and then we were startled by a rush of angry waters down the cabin staircase and into our berth under the door, gurgling and splashing from side to side of our little room as though bent on finding us some amusement and entertainment during the anything but 'silent' watches of the night. The captain told us that many times during the night the sides of the ship were lying in the sea, and that she sped through water at eleven or twelve knots an hour, and tried the strength of her timbers to the very utmost extent.

"This was a strange Sunday to us. Indeed, a greater contrast to Sabbaths at home I could scarcely imagine. We naturally put on Sunday attire, but nothing else around us marked the Sabbath's dawn. Many times during the day did one of the seamen come down into the cabin to bale and mop up the water, which came rushing down the staircase

THE VOYAGE (CONCLUDED). 57

like a cataract, and making quite as much noise. Our garments were dripping with water as we sat or stood in the cabin, and we felt no desire to face worse conditions out of doors.

"There was no opportunity for holding our usual service. After tea, in the cabin, we sang a few hymns, and tried to feel cheerful in the midst of our discomfort; but all hearts often stole away to our friends in England. We sat up until nearly midnight, holding firmly to the table to prevent ourselves from getting bruised heads on the one hand, and, by an opposite lurch, from being found in awkward positions half way across the table, which in spite of ourselves sometimes occurred, and caused a good deal of merriment. We remained thus long in the cabin, dreading the weary, restless hours we knew full well were before us.

"Verily our fears were well grounded. All, Mr. Wakefield included, declared they had never had such an experience. The storm of the previous day had, during the night, increased in fury, until I began seriously to think that the bulwarks of our ship would be stove in by the power of the waves and the heightening gale. The captain was on deck all night, giving orders in a voice that was clearly heard above the roar of the storm, while the excitement of our perilous position, joined with these things, induced a nervous feverishness which effectually banished all sleep from our eyes."

"Monday Morning, May 9th.—At half-past nine o'clock Mr. Wakefield ventured out of our little room, and found Mr. Yates and the mate standing against the steward's pantry, finishing their breakfast of cold porridge. They had tried sitting at the table in the cabin, but a 'sea' found its way through the skylight above them and drove them away. The captain had retired to rest, and I think the steward was lighting his fire, which had been twice put out that morning by the bursting in of the waters. He had himself, during the night, been twice washed out of his berth; but nevertheless had braved it out, 'not fearing,' as he said, 'to take cold from sea-water,' though his bed was completely soaked through. Mr. Wakefield got a little cold porridge for us, and we managed to breakfast in a rough sort of way; thankful moreover that sea-sickness had not again visited us, and laid us quite prostrate as before.

"' 'Tis a long storm that lasts for ever,' sailors say; and now we had passed its height. Towards noon a gleam of hope lighted up within us that calmer weather was approaching. Praise God for His preserving goodness! The captain, too, informed us that the glass was rising; and, between four and five o'clock in the afternoon, to our great joy the doors opening on to the deck were unfastened, and the gentlemen once more issued forth.

"At nine o'clock in the evening I was pressed to go up and see and enjoy a spot which really looked like a dry plank! We fully appreciated the lessening motion of the vessel, and the more tranquil state of 'old ocean;' although, at this time, we were making eight miles an hour. On retiring to our berth for the night, and peceiving the floor to be drying a little after the deluge of the past three or four days, my husband, with a long-drawn breath, and a depth of feeling I shall not soon forget, said 'Praise God!' Some of our friends at home might smile at such an expression of gratitude; but truly it found a ready response in my heart, and was no less strong than mutual. Oh what a luxury was that night's repose; and what lessons of thankfulness it taught for common mercies, after being for only a short time deprived of them. We have to-day made two hundred and thirty-one miles,—the longest distance the 'Emily' has ever travelled in twenty-four hours."

"Tuesday, May 10th.—By noon to-day the sun was out, and shining so warmly and brightly that I was tempted on deck, where I sat mending the gentlemen's gun-cases, while the captain put them through a drill exercise. The afternoon was taken up in exploring among the boxes in our berth, finding out the damage done, drying our things on deck, and getting our berths cleaned out and cleared up. In the evening Mr. Wakefield gave us a lesson in Sawahili.

"Just before tea, we saw a number of 'Cape pigeons' flying round and round our ship. They are very pretty birds, with white bodies, and long black wings, with white patches or spots on them. We tried to catch some with a hook and line baited with meat; but they saw the trick, and declined our hospitality. The mate says he has caught and eaten many of them.

"Numbers of the little 'stormy petrel,' or 'Mother Carey's chickens,' as the sailors call them, have for weeks accompanied our ship. They are about the size of a thrush, and have pretty white spotted wings. Sometimes they alight on the calm water in the wake of the ship, holding up their wings out of the wet, and riding over the waves like young ducks."

"Wednesday, May 11th.—The weather is becoming milder as our course is more northerly. It is now some days since we passed the longitude of the Cape of Good Hope; and we are now in the same latitude as Algoa Bay, but a good deal to the eastward. All our talk to the captain about the beauties of Capetown, and its rich supply of fruits and other luxuries, had no effect whatever in inducing him to near it and put in. I thought about an old schoolfellow, now the wife of a Church Missionary there, but was too far off to shake hands with her. One of the sailors said to me of Capetown, 'That is the place to go to; you would like living there much better than near Zanzibar, for it is not fit for a lady to live there.' He had been to Africa before, and as he said 'know a good deal about it.'"

"Friday, May 13th.—A bright, lovely, mild, sunny day, and quite reviving to our drooping spirits; more especially so as the vessel's movements are of a more tranquil kind, and not so disturbing to the inner man. Writing, reading, and walking on deck have occupied the whole day. The men have had a holiday to wash their clothes, and very busy they have been."

"Sunday Morning, May 15th.—About midnight, last night, a heavy swell rolled our vessel about tremendously, and immediately such a storm of thunder and lightning came on as the captain said he had never witnessed during the twenty-five years he had been at sea. It was truly terrific, and yet, at the same time, awfully grand. For at least twenty minutes, the most brilliant flashes of lightning followed each other in as quick succession as the movement of the eyelid in rapid winking. Not a second of time could be counted after one flash, before it was succeeded by another. The captain called to Mr. Wakefield to come on deck, as he would, perhaps, never see the like again; and, had it not been that he was suffering from a cold, he would much have enjoyed the sight. However, even through our small ground-glass skylight, the brilliancy of the flashes was almost dazzling to our sight, and made our little berth lighter than at noon-day. After that came the rising sea, which, like a midnight intruder, burst through all barriers, and rushed into our dominions with a noise like the smashing of half-a-dozen glass windows.

"We rose in the morning to find our little room in a very uncomfortable condition; but we have to learn a lesson of quiet resignation. There is still a heavy sea rolling; but the weather is fine. Service commenced on deck at the usual time, but was soon interrupted by a heavy shower of rain, which compelled us to seek shelter in the cabin. One of the men who had been reproved by the captain the night before, was not present at the service, and on being asked the reason why, said, he 'could not come in a right spirit.'

"We had the greatest difficulty in getting our dinner to-day, especially the soup; but no special calamity occurred, as each one undertook to watch some article beside his own plate, and so prevent its sudden leap on to the floor.

"In the afternoon, I finished reading the Rev. J. Townend's

THE VOYAGE (CONCLUDED).

Autobiography, and thought of the first Sabbath he spent in England, after his return from Australia, when I had the pleasure of seeing him at Exeter. After tea, we remained on deck, enjoying the beautiful moonlight, until it was time to retire. I then had an awkward fall: while I was standing by the companion ladder, the ship gave a sudden lurch, my feet slipped from under me, and down I fell, bruising my side against a corner with which I came into collision."

"Monday, May 16th.—Our eighty-first day at sea. At half-past one a.m., we were again roused by the shipping of seas, and the rolling of every movable thing in our berth on to the floor. We were obliged to get a light, pick up the books and other things, and make them as secure as possible. Without going further into detail, suffice it to say that the experiences of the previous Sunday night were as nearly as possible repeated; and, in consequence, I was unable to leave my berth until about noon. There was a heavy sea all day, with perpetual rolling of the ship, which proved a great hindrance to our writing or studying. There is no stepping on deck for me to-day, as the seas are constantly sweeping across the vessel from side to side, and our little ship has no poop."

"Wednesday, May 18th.—During the morning, as Mr. Wakefield and I felt a returning approach of sea-sickness, we went on deck to try the benefit of fresh air. All at once, a tremendous wave, at least twenty-five feet high, dashed over the side of the vessel; and, before we had time to do more than obtain a firm footing, and Mr. Wakefield to seize me firmly by the waist, an immense weight of water was thrown right over us, drenching us completely to the skin. I was wrapped in a thick woollen shawl; but, in a moment, everything was penetrated, and I was in a most pitiful plight, the water streaming down me as though I had just been lifted out of the sea. Mr. Wakefield was in exactly the same condition; and, after drawing a long breath, and slightly recovering from the shock, we disappeared below. What a fine laugh some of our good friends in England would have had at our expense, had they been eye-witnesses of the scene. Even Mr. Wakefield appeared delighted that I had been so beautifully caught. That very morning he had expressed a wish that I might get 'just one good sea' over me, so that I might know what it was like.

"The whole of the day was lost to us all, as far as writing or work of any kind was concerned; through our 'Emily' having a fresh attack of her old complaint, rolling over from side to side, as though trying her best to pitch everyone on deck overboard. We hope now to reach Zanzibar by the first of June."

"Thursday, May 19th.—A gentle breeze is carrying us along very smoothly, and on deck it is so nice and warm. How I do enjoy these fine quiet days! We have taken advantage of the fine warm day to dry our bedding and clothes in the sunshine. Everything in our berth moulds in a very short time. We are now rapidly approaching the end of our voyage, and are about 1,800 miles from Zanzibar.

"At four o'clock this afternoon, we met and spoke with a fine large vessel 'home-ward bound,'—from Madras to London. The passengers waved their handkerchiefs from the saloon windows, and we returned the greeting. The vessel's name was the 'Clarence,' and her captain used no signals. By voice he inquired 'What sort of weather on rounding the Cape?' to which our captain truly replied 'Strong south-westerly gales!' Having promised to report us, she was past, and time was exchanged by the usual signals. Then came the 'Good-bye,' expressed by raising and lowering the ensign three times: and by this time a long distance separated us. We have not seen so small a ship as our own since we left England."

"Friday, May 20th.—In the evening from six to eight o'clock, we were much interested in watching a grand display of lightning all round the south-western horizon. It

THE VOYAGE (CONCLUDED). 63

appeared behind a mass of dark clouds, stretching for a long distance, and looking like a thick forest resting on the sea. Behind this bank of clouds, it was playing, first in one place, and then in another, and then rushing from one end to the other it gleamed through the openings in the forest, and shed a flood of brilliancy upon the sky above. During the two hours we watched it, the flashes were never more than three or four seconds apart from each other; but to us it was quite unaccompanied by the sound of thunder."

"Sunday, May 22nd.—Our thirteenth Sabbath at sea. The bright, pleasant morning tempted us to take out our little sky-light, to let the fresh air into our berth. Alas, it was unwise; for immediately after breakfast, a heavy sea washed over the ship, and poured through the aperture into our sleeping apartment, drenching beds, books, clothes, and every other article which lay beneath. Oh, what a piece of work this made us, as everything had to be brought on deck to be dried, Sunday morning as it was.

"Our little vessel continued rolling and tossing with considerable violence, and we were compelled to hold Divine service in the cabin. Mr. Yates preached; and referred to the probability of its being the last time he should address the little assembly.

"We are now making rapid progress north-wards, having entered the Mozambique channel. Yesterday we travelled two hundred miles, and we are hoping to reach Zanzibar to-morrow week, and in this good prospect we rejoice."

"Monday, May 23rd.—We have experienced a very sudden and great change in the temperature. The mate felt the heat so much as to decline coming down into the cabin to dinner. Every one who did appeared to be in a melting condition, and pocket handkerchiefs were freely used. The captain remarked to Dado that it was of little use giving *him* pea-soup, for he had no sooner taken it than it oozed out again through the pores of his skin."

"Tuesday, May 24th.—The heat is still rising, and we

are all incapacitated for work. The thermometer stands at 82 in our berth.

"This morning we were entertained by a conversation our captain had with the captain of a French vessel, the 'Lotus,' bound for a port on the north of Madagascar, and thence to Zanzibar. He asked us to report him. There were two negroes on board his ship, a great deal darker than Dado, dressed in pure white jackets, and without caps. Dado did not at all care to recognise them, or show any more of his face than he could help. I noticed him pulling his cap down over his eyes, and looking very demure.

"Last Thursday, we were opposite Natal; but quite out of sight of land. I did not at the time forget my dear friend who left Birmingham in 1866, to become the wife of the Rev. S. H. Stott, Wesleyan Missionary, and who is now resident at Natal. I told the captain how delighted I should be if we could just 'put in' and see her; but he only smiled, and steered ahead. 'May God bless and preserve her, and make her abundantly useful in the cause of her Saviour and Lord,' was my silent prayer."

"Friday, May 27th.—On our rising this morning the thermometer stood at 85, and during the day the heat increased. There appears to be a dead calm resting on the waters. Not a breath of wind is stirring, and at night the sea looks like a lake, and the clouds on the distant horizon like the shores of it all studded with trees. The current, however, has carried us seventy miles in the right direction during the last twenty-four hours; for which we feel thankful. We are now about five hundred miles from Zanzibar."

"Sunday, May 29th.—Our fourteenth, and, we hope, during this voyage, our last Sabbath on the ocean.

"During the last few evenings the constellations in the heavens have been very bright; millions of stars of varied brilliancy adorning a blue and cloudless sky above us, and calling for our admiration as we sit on deck, in the cool of the evening, 'All Thy works praise Thee, O Lord, and Thy saints bless Thee.'

"Having yesterday derived much benefit by being on deck about six a.m., I again thought to enjoy another glorious sunrise; but found, on reaching the top of the cabin staircase, that his solar majesty was just peeping above the horizon; and he looked me out of countenance at once. Presently, however, he disappeared behind a broad belt of clouds of lovely form, tinging their edges with his glory, and the sky all around with an indescribable radiance of varied beauty and colour, on which I was able to gaze with delight and admiration.

"The sea was calmer than ever, and like a vast expanse of oil lying unmoved and undisturbed by the slightest breath of wind.

"At 11-20, our last service was commenced on deck, and all hands were present. Mr. Wakefield preached from 'So He bringeth them to their desired haven; O that men would praise the Lord for His goodness, and for his wonderful works to the children of men.' Psalm cvii. 30, 31.

"In the evening Mr. Wakefield and I joined in a few favourite hymns before retiring to rest."

"Monday, May 30th.—I again rose to watch the dawn of day, and the sun's rising. The water was slightly ruffled on its surface, and showed some promise of a breeze, which our captain is most intensely desiring.

"Some of us had been hoping to have some amusement in fishing up all manner of curiosities from the calm water,— bits of seaweed, leaves of trees, nuts, and small floating jelly and shell fish, large quantities of which were now floating past; but the breeze disappointed us of this pleasure. At twelve, noon, it was ascertained that the current had again carried us along for seventy miles, although we had appeared to be all the time at a standstill. I felt this to be cause for much thankfulness, and it was quite a surprise for us all."

"Thursday morning, May 31st.—There is a nice breeze

F

carrying us along at about five miles an hour. To-day we gave up the hope of reaching Zanzibar by the 1st of June as anticipated. A large number of beautiful fish are playing round the ship; but we cannot catch them."

"Wednesday, June 1st.—Our ninety-sixth day at sea. Early this morning we were again visited by fish, but of a much larger kind. 'A shark! a shark!' was the cry; and we rushed on deck to see this much-dreaded fish. Presently a second, and then a third, were seen playing in front of our ship, all beautifully marked over their brown backs with irregular patches of white. Three, five, six, seven, were counted, and soon the sea all around us seemed alive with them, jumping and splashing about as if they expected a good breakfast being thrown to them.

"At half-past ten o'clock this morning we sighted land! The shore of East Africa.

"I can scarcely describe my feelings as for the first time I looked upon the edge of that great continent, or rather island, on which I was so soon to set my foot and make my home. Tears came to my eyes, and a choking sensation was felt in my throat as a thousand different thoughts rushed into my mind. Then and there, while standing leaning over the side of the ship with my face to the westward, I gave up myself afresh to God, body, soul, and spirit; and prayed Him to fit me to work for Him, and to use me for His glory, should He see fit to spare my life. The following hymn of Charles Wesley expressed the feeling and language of my heart at this time,—

> 'Lord, in the strength of grace,
>   With a glad heart and free,
> Myself, my residue of days
>   I consecrate to Thee.
>
> Thy ransomed servant I
>   Restore to Thee thine own;
> And, from this moment, live or die
>   To serve my God alone.

"At one p.m. Monfia Island appeared in sight, and by the use of the opera glass we could discern trees all along its banks thick with foliage. This Island is twenty-eight miles long. We passed it about six o'clock in the evening.

"We now began to make preparations for leaving the ship, as we expected to anchor between eight and nine o'clock next morning. After working very hard at packing our loose things in empty cases given us by the captain, I went to bed as tired as could be, having arranged that we should be called at five a.m. to finish our preparations for going ashore. But I was too excited to sleep, and at half-past one got up to breathe a little fresh air, as our berth was almost stifling. Having lain down again I found on next rising that it wanted a quarter to three, and I retired again, sighing for the dawn of day. At length the night passed away."

"Thursday, June 2nd.—As soon as it was day we went on deck to see the land, and found that the south end of the Island of Zanzibar was visible. Then we returned to our packing. Oh how excited and talkative everybody was. We could not get on with our preparations for being constantly called up on deck to see something or other. First a fishing boat could be discerned in the distance on its way into port, and the captain was anxious to seize the first opportunity of getting some one to point out the passage among the reefs and small islands which lie about Zanzibar. Then I was called up to see some rocks of curious formation, rising like immense mushrooms out of the sea. Then to come and look at the cocoa-nut trees lining the shore, and find them exactly like one has seen them in pictures, but producing different feelings. Now I am told a native boat or canoe is near with coloured men in it, and Mr. Wakefield is desired by the captain to ask them to draw near. At first they are afraid, and keep at a respectful distance, but on Mr. Wakefield promising, in Sawahili, to give them five dollars to show us the way into Zanzibar, they are soon tumbling over the side of the vessel, chattering in a tongue that only themselves and Mr. Wakefield understand, and which simply amuses the rest of us.

"My first feeling towards these poor naked creatures was one of pity and commiseration for their desolate and miserable condition. Their only garment was a narrow strip of dirty calico, about half a yard deep, fastened round the loins. Their hair was shaven quite close, and their skin, which was of a dark brown colour, seemed to cover only a lot of bones. Poor things! they appeared to be half starved, and ate with much eagerness some pieces of biscuit and a piece of heavy bread, which had been laid aside, and was quite mouldy.

"About half-past one o'clock the Zanzibar pilot came on board to conduct us to our anchorage, about one mile distant. He was a short, thick-set man, and was in full dress. This consisted of a richly-embroidered silk skirt; a blue jacket, ornamented with gold and silver thread; a white shirt front, with a great deal of needlework about it; a costly belt of silver, to which a dagger in a silver case is suspended, and to crown all, a dignified-looking turban of white cloth, striped with red. He conversed with me quite fluently in English.

"We anchored near the powder magazine, about two miles from Zanzibar, where the forty tons of gunpowder taken in at Gravesend had to be discharged. The captain and the pilot now went ashore, leaving us to dine, and to await any message from Mr. Wakefield's friends who were expecting to see us.

"It was about two o'clock in the afternoon of Thursday, June 2nd, when the loud rattling of the anchor chain told us that our voyage was over. About four o'clock we were glad to see a boat nearing the ship. It was rowed by two black boys in white jackets and scarlet caps, and a clerical-looking gentleman was sitting at the helm. Mr. Wakefield thought at first that it was Bishop Tozer, but on the boat coming nearer he found he was mistaken. The gentleman was soon on deck, and introduced himself as Mr. Pennell, of the

English Universities' Mission. He gave us a hearty welcome to Zanzibar, and presented my husband with a letter from Bishop Tozer, of which the following is a copy:—

"'Shangain House, English Mission, Zanzibar, May 17th, 1870.—My dear Mr. Wakefield,—I am leaving this letter to welcome you back to Africa on the eve of my departure for the coast. We have made arrangements for taking you and Mrs. Wakefield and Mr. Yates, and your Galla boy in at the Mission House, where you will find rooms prepared for your reception. I only regret that I am not myself able to assist at your landing. Pray make up your minds to take sufficient rest before starting for Mombas. I do not propose being absent more than a month, even if so long, and I shall be cruelly disappointed to miss you. I do not think there is any house in the town where you can be taken in with less inconvenience than here, and I am sure there is none where your sojourn will give the inmates so much pleasure. Believe me, with kind regards to your party, my dear Mr. Wakefield,

Always yours sincerely,

WILLIAM GEORGE TOZER,

Rev. T. Wakefield.'   Missionary Bishop.

"Praised be our heavenly Father for all His goodness to us in providing for us so kind a welcome to a comfortable home at the end of our long journey, and that we are well in health. I felt almost overcome by this expression of disinterested hospitality to so large a party of us, to the greater part of whom the good Bishop was a stranger.

"While we were waiting for the captain's return, Mr. Pennell told us a sad story of a visitation of cholera in January last. No less than 10,000 people had died in the town of Zanzibar alone, and 50,000 or 60,000 others in the island and along the coast, until there was no place to bury them. It was at first arranged that we should have come out in the steam-ship 'Malta.' When this vessel arrived at

Zanzibar the cholera was at its height. Several of the crew were at once attacked, and died. When the steamer left she carried the disease away with her, and by the time she again arrived at Suez nearly all on board were dead. A gracious Providence arranged that we should miss the 'Malta,' and live.

> 'He leadeth me, O blessed thought,
> O words with Heavenly comfort fraught;
> Whate'er I do, where'er I be,
> Still 'tis *God's* hand that leadeth me.'

And I would acknowledge at this time, and praise Him for His goodness to us, in preserving us from this great danger.

"At length the captain returned to the ship, bringing with him a Mr. Donaldson, who handed round to us the longed-for letters from home. And now for the first time in my life it was my privilege to see the full meaning of that text in the Proverbs, 'As cold waters to a thirsty soul, so is good news from a far country.'

"Less welcome, but very refreshing, were some green oranges and loaves of nice white bread, of which however I could scarcely eat for very joy.

"Leaving the 'Emily,' we soon rounded a point of sand, and then gradually the town of Zanzibar came into view. The European houses, which are large white buildings, stretch along the shore at a short distance from the water's edge. They have flat roofs, are generally turretted, and either built of white stone or stuccoed and whitewashed. They look very pretty at a distance, and, with their massive architecture, somewhat imposing. Besides these European houses we saw a number of native huts, poor, low, hovel-like places, roofed with a coarse-looking thatch, which I afterwards found is the dried palm leaf.

"We landed at the first of the large whitewashed houses, and very nice it was to feel that our feet were really upon firm ground once more. A large number of boys from the Mission School were standing on the beach ready to carry in our luggage, and beside these we observed three smiling white faces. They all welcomed us with great kindness, and in a little time we found ourselves in a fine, large, cool, airy room, about twenty-five feet long and fourteen wide.

"At six o'clock we took tea, our first meal in Africa; and the piled up dishes of bananas and oranges, which were such ornaments to the table, served another purpose also. There was no lady in the house; but Mr. Pennell and Mr. Morton, who did duty one at each end of the table, in a kind and obliging manner, almost made me forget this. The room was an upper one, and had six windows looking out upon the bay, and, as we sat at tea, we had a splendid view. In the harbour four or five of the Sultan's 'men of war' were riding at anchor, and a number of Arab dhows and small fishing boats filled up the scene. Along the beach, and almost immediately under our windows, paced to and fro men and women of every colour and of every clime. As all the windows were open a splendid breeze came in and fanned our hot cheeks, and so my first impressions of Zanzibar were very agreeable.

"After tea my husband went out to make a few calls, and at half-past eight Mr. Yates, Dado, and I attended the reading of prayers in the English Church; and the minister at our desire returned public thanks to God for His goodness to us during our long and now safely-ended voyage."

CHAPTER VII.

Zanzibar and its People.

BEING now comfortably settled at the English Church Mission House, Zanzibar, Mrs Wakefield embraced every opportunity presented of becoming acquainted with the new and strange people among whom she expected to remain until an opportunity presented itself to the Mission party of proceeding to their destination at Ribé, a hundred and forty miles distant. Her introduction to the sights and sounds of Zanzibar shall be described in her own words.

"On the afternoon of the day following our landing, Mr. Wakefield took me out for my first walk in Zanzibar. I shall never forget it. The streets are not more than eight or nine feet wide, and are very crooked and uneven; and the confinement is so oppressive that one wonders when one shall come to a wide opening, or to a square, so as for a moment to be able to breathe freely. The entrances to all the European houses here are very much alike. You pass first under a wide gateway into a square court yard, then up a flight of stone steps,—sometimes under cover and sometimes not—on to the first floor. The ground floor is never used as a dwelling-house; but is set apart for stores and lumber of all kinds. After making our first call, we passed down one of the leading thoroughfares of the town, about eight feet wide. Squatted in every doorway, were men and women of a great variety of shades of colour and styles of costume. Some were profusely decorated with jewelry, and had large rings in their ears and noses, of pure gold or silver. Others had silver wire wrapped round their toes, looking like so many rings, and large massive ornaments round their ankles. Some wore turbans of various bright colours, and had red silk caps, embroidered like smoking caps. The chief article of dress was a long sort of white calico night-gown not coming up close to the neck, and with short sleeves : no shoes or stockings, of course. We had nearly passed out of the street before I perceived that all these people were the principal shop-keepers of the place. However, on peeping into the dark places as we passed, I observed two or three shelves with articles on them of a most miscellaneous description— rolls of coloured calico, red pocket handkerchiefs, earthenware basins, drugs in bottles, oranges, bananas, a few strings of beads, a basket of rice, or millet, etc.; but I was too much taken up in looking at the dark faces around me to peer much into their dark little dwellings.

"The people seemed quite as much interested in me as I was in them, and forgot their business of trading in their eagerness to take stock of the stranger who had so suddenly appeared among them. We soon gathered a train of followers, who chatted away to one another all the while, stopping when we stopped, and moving on when we did the same, and looking unutterable things when I spoke in an unknown tongue.

"At length we reached the market-place, where corn, fruit, and vegetables were being offered for sale. Here such crowds gathered round me, that I began to feel a little nervous ; so Mr. Wakefield went on before, calling out, 'Simillah! simillah!' 'Make way! make way!' and the word was quickly passed from lip to lip as the people fell back on either side to allow me to pass; feeling of and stroking my dress, however, as I went by. I thought of a Punch and Judy show in England, and was much amused at being considered a 'sight,' for such crowds of men, women, and children. Most of them smiled upon me, and some ventured the usual salutation 'Yambo,' that is, 'How are you,' and when I said in reply, 'Yambo sana,' they were gratified exceedingly.

"There is a strange mixture of population in Zanzibar. There first meets you the dignified Arab, dressed in long costly robes and bright turban; then the fairer and intelligent looking Hindoo; then a number of more than half naked Sawahili slaves, in pairs, carrying a burden on a pole, and jabbering something most unintelligible as they pass you by. Then there are Portuguese, dressed European fashion; Goanese, and I must not forget among others, the Banyans, or British Hindoo subjects. I shall not soon forget Banyan-street; because there, a number of the sacred cows of the Hindoos were wandering up and down at pleasure, putting their noses unrestrained into the shopkeepers' baskets, and eating whatever they were disposed. These cows are milked, but no one dares to kill them for food; and, as the streets are very narrow, we kept rubbing against these smooth-skinned pretty creatures as we passed along.

"The Hindoos seemed to wear the greatest number of ornaments. I saw a little child in the arms of its nurse, wearing a pinafore of crimson satin, covered with spangles. The little one had also rings in her ears; and massive silver rings on her ankles, which I could not help thinking were in danger of making the child a cripple for life. In another doorway I saw a girl about sixteen years old, with five large rings in each ear; and to each ring a drop was attached, as large as a lady's thimble. She had also a ring in her nose, which, as it hung lower than her bottom lip, would, I thought, be a great inconvenience to her when eating.

"On our way home we met a fair little English girl, with light curly hair, who was taking a ride on a pony, accompanied by her negro man-nurse. What a contrast her fair face presented to those of the swarthy and ebony ones of the multitudes around. We stopped and kissed her

THE OLD BRITISH CONSULATE, ZANZIBAR.

smiling, pale little face, and found that she was the daughter of Dr. and Mrs. Kirk, of the English consulate."

"Saturday, June 4th.—I have passed a most restless and uncomfortable night; and the reason is, that those dreadful mosquitoes have been paying me such 'marked' attention. My hands and arms are stung all over; and bright red spots everywhere abound. I heard the church bell at six o'clock, calling us up to prayers; but I was too tired to rise so early. Prayers commence at half-past six, and the Mission people attend; but the European residents, generally, do not feel so far interested as to do so.

"After breakfast Mr. Wakefield and I again went to the market, to see it at its busiest time. On the way we saw men and women carrying baskets of fruit and vegetables on their heads to go to the market-place for sale. The large open space devoted to buying and selling was all astir with a curious, mixed multitude of coloured people of all shades. In one corner was a herd of goats for sale. In another spot a native auctioneer was selling a quantity of Indian corn, which lay on a mat on the ground before him. It was interesting to watch his earnestness, as, in a loud tone, he rapidly repeated the different bids; and, to see him looking round with as quick an eye as an English gentleman of the same calling, to catch the nod of intending purchasers was truly amusing.

"The fruit offered for sale is usually piled up on a mat spread on the ground, and often on the same mat little heaps of bananas, oranges, &c., are laid together, so many for a pie (halfpenny), as on the apple stalls and barrows in London. About five or six oranges are sold for a pie, and as many bananas. The natives were much amused to see us stand and eat our mango, and gathered round us on all sides, until we found quite a difficulty in getting away from their midst. As we passed along the same curiosity was manifested as on the previous evening. Three or four Sawahili men followed us about for an hour or two, calling out to everyone in our path to 'get out of the lady's way,' and making remarks about everything we paused to examine, in a most officious manner. One of them could speak a very little English and constantly kept airing it. I think they expected we should give them a few pice for their 'services.'

"My husband took me inside one or two shops kept by Goanese. They are the most respectable establishments in the place; but even these have to get all their light from the doorway. In these shops there is a little of almost everything: drapery, haberdashery, drugs, earthenware, sweets, wines, preserved fruits, preserved meats from Europe in sealed tins, etc., for all of which articles they demand exceedingly high prices. These Goanese speak English very well.

"On our way home we called at the English consulate to see Dr. and Mrs. Kirk, and to register ourselves as British subjects, a form which is necessary if we wish for protection in this Mohammedan country."

"Monday, June 6th.—Yesterday the morning service was held at seven o'clock, and consisted of the reading of the Liturgy and the celebration of the Lord's Supper. The congregation was composed, first, of the boys of the Mission School, about forty in number, who all live on the Mission premises, the three young English teachers who are employed by the Mission, and ourselves. Before the service was over Miss Pakeman, an English lady, and about sixteen native girls who live in another house about two miles away in the country, augmented the congregation. About twenty of the boys were dressed in scarlet gowns with white muslin surplices over them, and walked into church in procession behind the minister. First of all, however, a boy carried a long cross at the head of the procession, and during the service lighted candles stood on the altar. The wine was mixed with water, and what remained in the consecrated vessels was drunk by the minister kneeling at the altar.

It was Whit-Sunday. The boys sing very sweetly, and seem to have a very good idea both of time and tune.

"The Sabbath evening service was held at six o'clock. The Rev. Mr. Pennell officiated. He referred to the presence of Mr. Wakefield; and said that it was rather remarkable that on returning to the work of Christ in East Africa, his first Sabbath on shore should be Whit-Sunday, and trusted he would go forward whither he was sent full of the Holy Ghost and of power. No native residents were present at the service, and the mission is apparently confined to the instruction and training of the boys and girls before referred to, with a view of their becoming teachers and missionaries to their own people. Most of the people of Zanzibar are Mohammedans, and no one ever expects to make any converts from among them.

"In the evening, about eight or nine o'clock, the moon being up, we went on to the flat roof of the house and sat for an hour or more enjoying the soft, cool breeze. The tops of the neighbouring houses were also occupied in the same way; while here and there persons were promenading to and fro in quiet conversation. Some of the Europeans have little towers built on the house-tops, as 'look outs' for their expected vessels.

"What a calm, delightful Sabbath evening this was to me. Blessed be God for all His loving-kindness and watchful care over us. How safe we might always feel, did we but remember what an Almighty arm is stretched around us for our protection."

"Tuesday, June 7th.—This morning Mr. W. and I and Mr. Yates went out to make some more calls. The first person we called upon was 'French Charlie.' This man keeps the largest retail store in Zanzibar, and is the only butcher and bread-baker in the town. He came out as a steward in a vessel, and, commencing business here, soon made his fortune. We pay fivepence for a little round loaf, such as we should pay a penny or three half-pence for at home, and it is anything but *solid*. It would be a fine speculation for some baker at home to come out here and carry on a similar business.

"After drinking a glass of 'Charlie's' rose coloured sherbet, we met with Bukhett, the pilot of the port, who said we must go with him to see his house. We found his 'state room' full of all kinds of European ornaments, as vases, glass and china, pictures, mirrors, etc., all of which he seemed very proud to show us. Here again we had to drink rose sherbet, and, on leaving, he gave me a native fan.

"On walking through the streets, we frequently stopped to look at the various articles offered for sale; and very curious were some of the women to know who I was, frequently making my husband laugh by their remarks. One of them asked him if I were his daughter. It was noon before we reached home, and the sun was exceedingly powerful. This however is the 'cool season,' the most favourable time in which we could have landed.

"Yesterday, a python, or boa constrictor, was lying on the beach, quite dead. It had swallowed some poor man's goat, and then, being utterly helpless, was easily killed. The man had carried it to the sea shore to exhibit it, hoping to get sufficient money from the passers by to cover his loss. It was twelve feet long, and, where not swollen out, about as thick as a man's arm."

"Wednesday, June 8th.—I have spent this day at Dr. Kirk's. Before dinner Mr. Pennell called to take me to visit an Arab lady, the wife of a Sheik, or Arab nobleman. The appointment having been previously made, the lady (or bibi, pronounced beebee,) met us at the door, and shook hands, with the usual salutation of 'Yambo;' and I was then conducted into the reception room. It was long, narrow, and lofty, and the walls looked as if they had not been whitewashed for years, and presented a strange contrast to the dress of the lady. I was placed in a comfortable arm-chair, and she sat in another on my left, and close by me.

The Sheik sat on my right, on a kitanda, or native bedstead, something like a long four-legged stool, covered with a beautifully worked mat. As I did not know a word of Arabic, Mr. Pennell was allowed to be present as interpreter. I was told through him that they were exceedingly glad to see me; that the bibi had never seen an English lady before; and that she was much interested at the whiteness of my hand, which she kept stroking all the time, as well as examining my dress minutely from top to toe. Her dress was of crimson satin, beautifully embroidered with gold and silver thread, and coloured silks. It was made without any fulness in the skirt, and was just short enough to display her bare feet and massively beautiful anklets, which however, reminded me of a captive's fetters, in spite of their glitter and value. Her bracelets were of red beads, set in gold. Over her head, and fastened under her chin with a very large drooping ornament, was a coloured silk handkerchief, doubled square and crossed over the left shoulder.

"She was smiling all the time, and never took her eyes off me for a moment. I could not see how her hair was dressed, but it *was* hair, and not wool. She said it was not the custom for Arab ladies to go out in the day time, but that she would be pleased to return the visit some evening, after dark. She told me she prayed to God five times every day, and could read the Koran, but had not been taught to understand it. The Sheik said he had hurt his shoulder, and asked me to pray that it might soon get well. He liked the English, he continued, better than any other Europeans, and flattered us exceedingly. He was clad in a long white gown, and apologised for being in undress, by saying he could not appear in any other costume in the presence of his wife.

"Before we left, two daughters were introduced. They appeared to be about sixteen and eighteen years old. They did nothing but laugh, and say I was the first white lady they had seen. They were dressed in the same style as their mother; but less expensively.

"And now the servants brought in sherbet for us. I was obliged to refer to Mr. Pennell, as to the proper etiquette of the occasion. We took a glass of the sherbet, and then coffee was brought in. Of this I was directed to take three cups. The cups were exceedingly small, without handles, and being too hot to be held were placed in useful little holders, like egg cups. The servants kept handing us very small, and very thin slices of bread, cut with a penknife, and which made our fingers very sticky, as the cake or hallua was more like soft toffy than anything else. After this another little tray was handed to us, full of cups of sweetened milk, very nice, and of which I was expected to take two. Lastly, a little slave boy brought in a silver vessel, shaped like a large bottle, filled with rose water; from the perforated stopper of which the bibi saturated my handkerchief, and perfumed my dress.

"At seven o'clock in the evening Mrs. Kirk called, by previous appointment, to accompany me to see the ladies of the Sultan's Prime Minister. The Mahommedan religion allows every man four wives, and Sheik S—— lives up to his privilege in this respect. We were introduced to three of the four. The Sheik met us at the bottom of the staircase, and the ladies were standing at the top to receive us. We were shown into a magnificently furnished apartment, more like an English drawing-room than anything else. There were mirrors on all sides, and six paraffin lamps were burning brightly in different parts of the room. The Sheik sat down with us, and the ladies laughed and chatted so merrily that it was quite pleasant to see and hear them, although I could not understand the conversation. Their dress was much more costly than that of the lady I saw in the morning, and their ornaments much more numerous. They were younger too, and the beauty of one of them especially attracted my attention. I think they were Circassian girls, from eighteen

G

to twenty years old, and were almost as fair as English people. They all wore gold coronets of different patterns, and many earrings hung one above another, some of which were large enough for bracelets, and as thick as a slate pencil. Their arms were covered almost to the elbow with bracelets. One wore nose-jewels, and had also a necklace of gold medals hanging quite down to her waist in front. The pretty one, the youngest, played us some lively airs on the violin, which she made to sound very much like the Scotch bag-pipe. The others, who cannot play, were chaffing and laughing at the player all the time, and trying to 'put her out.' Although the Sheik was present, there did not seem to be the least restraint; and, as they are never allowed to go outside the door, they may possibly enjoy their life better together than if they were alone.

"We drank sherbet and coffee, and inspected the albums; in which were some of the most splendid cartes I ever saw; chiefly of the sovereigns of Europe, and their families. They were preparing to show us a number of stereographs, piles of which lay on the table; but as we thought we should be kept too long, we rose to depart. They all walked along the verandah with us to the head of the staircase; then shook hands with us, and the Sheik politely saw us home."

"Friday, June 10th.—We have been very busy to-day, looking after the landing of our luggage; counting the boxes, etc. It is very amusing to hear the monotonous singing of the natives, while carrying burdens. It consists just of two or three words repeated over and over again. They brought my piano in very carefully. Ropes were slung underneath and hung on two poles, which rested on the shoulders of eight men. I asked Mr. Wakefield what it was they were saying, and it was 'plenty of meat,' 'plenty of meat.' To-day is the Mahommedan Sabbath. The Sultan's flag is flying over the palace, and on all the dhows and men of war in the harbour. Ships of other nations also pay deference to the day by hoisting theirs. Even on shore, I see a large British ensign waving from the top of the consulate."

"Saturday, June 11th.— In the morning, I went to Dr. Christie's to offer my services as nurse, both the doctor and Mrs. C. being prostrate with fever. In these cases the native servants are of but little use. They often think it too much trouble to go into their mistress's room to announce visitors; and in every possible way shirk their duty.

"At half-past six we went to the American consulate to a dinner party, and during the evening I learned a circumstance that afresh made my heart overflow with gratitude to God for the safety with which we had accomplished our voyage. A gentleman called in to see Captain Webb while we were at dinner, who told us the following facts. He and his wife had just arrived from England. Just before our passage in the 'Emily' was engaged, he and his wife had gone to look at her, but seeing the limited accommodation she offered they declined subjecting themselves to so many inconveniences, and engaged a passage in another vessel. They proceeded safely until off the island of Monfia, about a day's sail from Zanzibar, when the ship was wrecked on a reef, and went to pieces; and all that was saved of their goods was the clothes they stood before us in. I afterwards had some conversation with this gentleman, who seemed very pleased to meet with us. He had heard of our having engaged passages in the little 'Emily,' and had often wondered during their own voyage how 'the lady' was getting on. I told him what those on board had told me: *viz.*, that they thought I should not survive the passage, etc. But here I am, quite restored to health, and surrounded with every comfort. Blessed be God. I ought not now to talk of past distresses, but rather to praise God for my kind reception at Zanzibar. Bless the Lord, O my soul."

"Sunday, June 12th.—At seven a.m., we attended Divine Service. The mornings are so delightfully cool and pleasant out here, that it is a perfect treat to be up early to enjoy them. The celebration of the Lord's Supper takes place every Sabbath morning here, but to-day none of the boys remained. After breakfast, Mr. Pennell walked out to the Shamba, where the girls live, to conduct a service for them, and returned just in time to preach here at six in the evening."

"Monday morning, June 13th.—Mr. Wakefield has been out to see about a boat for Mombas, and we are to be informed by the custom-house officials as soon as an opportunity offers for our conveyance. It is very pleasant staying at Zanzibar, among so many kind friends; but we are anxious to reach our own home, and get to work. The rest here has been very acceptable, and has done us all good. Dado goes to school with the boys here, and seems thoroughly at home among them. The Sunday dress of the girls consists of a plain white frock, and a sort of red cap, as if a red handkerchief were put tight over the head, and all the four corners tucked in behind, making a sort of sham chignon, although in reality their hair is as short and woolly as that of the boys. I have not yet seen them in the week-day dress, but we are invited to go out to the Shamba shortly.

"The good Bishop and his attendants have just arrived home from their journey into the interior, after travelling all night by the brilliant light of the full moon. The Bishop has for some days been suffering from fever, and had to be carried on a native bedstead. At first he had eight men, so as to have a change of hands; but, before they had got far, one of them ran away, and so, every time they rested, there was a noisy quarrel as to who should take the extra turn; and the poor invalid lay helpless on the earth, until the dispute was settled. The Bishop was well enough to come in to dinner, and, as he entered the room, he gave us all a most cordial and hearty welcome, and though he was far from well, he enlivened us all by his cheerful and sprightly conversation."

"Monday night.—At five o'clock this afternoon, I was

honoured by a presentation to Said Majid, the Sultan of Zanzibar, at the Royal Palace.

"Dr. Kirk kindly allowed one of his servants to go with me as interpreter, and the Sultan's Prime Minister called to escort me to the palace. As we deliberately walked through the streets, everybody stepped forward, and laying their right hand horizontally across the breast, made their bow of obeisance, uttering at the same time some words I did not understand; the Sheik in every case returning the salutation. On passing the fort a company of soldiers defiled out and formed two long lines between which we walked, while each soldier bowed as we passed. On arriving at the palace another escort awaited us, and I was conducted to the top of a staircase. Here, the Sultan himself stood to welcome me with a cordial English-like shake of the hand. He then conducted me along the verandah into a large lofty room or hall, the floor of which was paved with polished white marble. We walked along the centre of this room to the opposite end, where two chairs were placed, on one of which I was desired to be seated, and the Sultan took the other, close beside me. He conversed with me very kindly, told me about the 'Sea-king' which is to sail to-morrow, carrying a mail; about his small house at Mombas; that he had a beautiful residence at Dar Salam, to which he is going on Thursday next, and invited me to pay him a visit there. Cups of coffee were brought in similar to those I have before described, and afterwards glasses of sherbet.

"The Sultan's wives were now admitted. They came into the room in that peculiar Arab dress of all colours, but with the addition of gold masks which partly hid their faces from view, the top of them passing like a band across their forehead, and a similar band passing across the middle of the face, joined at each end to a perpendicular piece which connected the two. I told them I liked Zanzibar very well, and they said I had better remain here, instead of going to Mombas, as it is much pleasanter. To this I replied that I must go where 'Bwana' Wakefield went, and they laughed heartily.

"On rising to leave, my handkerchief was taken by the attendant, and returned to me highly perfumed with otto of roses. Only two ladies were introduced to me, and they had both dark skins. The Sultan said the other one was sick. They both shook hands with me, and so did the Sultan, who said 'Good-bye' to me at the place where he met me on entering.

"I found the Prime Minister waiting to see me home, and the same marked respect was paid to him by every one we met as before, and he did not leave me until I came to the gate of the mission house."

CHAPTER VIII.

Lights and Shadows.

IN the island of Zanzibar, as in most tropical countries, are seen, side by side, and in the closest proximity, those striking contrasts of loveliness and deformity, pleasure, and pain, luxury and want, high manly independence and mean crouching servility, healthful enjoyment of life, and the most terrible forms of disease and death which render it at once a most delightful and a most disagreeable place of residence for Europeans. With some of these contrasts, Mrs. Wakefield was now becoming acquainted, and her account of them is presented to the reader in this chapter.

"A few days ago, Mr. Wakefield took me for my first walk into the country behind Zanzibar, and a more delightful ramble could not be desired by those who enjoy a grassy path, and the sight of beautiful, rich verdure all around. It reminded me very much of a walk through the meadows at Mountsorrel. There was, however, one thing to mar our pleasure, which was the sight of human bones, skulls, back and rib bones, and sometimes a nearly whole skeleton, lying here and there close by our path. During the prevalence of the cholera, in January, many of the victims were carried out of the city to the Mnazi Mmoja, as this place is called, and thrown down among the bushes without burial; while in other cases, a shallow trench was dug, and the bodies, scarcely covered with soil, fell a ready prey to the wild dogs, which abound here, and which came night after night to enjoy the horrid feast.

"We crossed over this plain, which at high tide is completely inundated, and entered a narrow lane, all covered with fine soft green grass, delightfully cool and pleasant to the tread, and which divided two plantations. On either side of us rose high spreading green hedgerows, strongly reminding me of the lovers' walks in Devonshire, only the foliage was of a softer and fresher green.

"I gathered some very pretty wild flowers. Some of them were much like the English sweet pea, and were both white and coloured. Others were in shape like the convolvulus, some yellow and others blue.

"Soon we found ourselves passing by a grove of orange trees, all laden with fruit, the boughs drooping far over the pathway with its weight. Only one orange here and there had a tinge of yellow, the rest were of a dark rich green; but even in this state they looked luxuriant, and I stood gazing around me with delight. There were lemon trees, and limes too, and far above these the feathery palm tree proudly raised its head, its fine rich plumes waving gracefully in the breeze, underneath which clustered crowds of the young cocoa-nuts, the outside rind being still green. At present, fruit is not very plentiful. The orange season is not considered to be here until July or August, when the fruit is quite ripe. Mr. Wakefield says we must come over early some morning when the owners are here and get permission to rove about in the groves, and pluck and eat as we like. He has often done this. There is usually a nice little arbour or summer-house in the centre of the grove, where it would be delightful to sit and rest.

"Many of the trees we passed on our walk appeared in the distance like English oaks or elms when in full, fresh leaf; tall, stately, and with fine large trunks. Oh, how I wished I could show the picture to my dear friends at home. Description is impossible.

"We passed a Hindu cemetery, full of white stone tombs, with long grass growing between. We also met great numbers of native men and women, in long white garments, or with only a cloth round the loins, carrying baskets of fruit, and singing as they went along. Many of the girls have a very fantastic way of dressing their hair, which is short and curly. They divide it into horizontal stripes from front to back, by partings an inch or so from each other, and make one long curl of the hair between, running right over the head. We reached home at sundown."

"Tuesday, June 14th.—We have to-day been very busy, packing a little box, and finishing our letters for dear, dear old England. With my dear Aunt Fidler I would say,—

> 'I all on earth forsake
> Its wisdom, fame, and power;
> And HIM my only portion make,
> My shield and tower.'"

"Wednesday, June 15th.—On the morning of this day, Mr. Wakefield and I went by invitation to spend a few days with Miss Pakeman, at the Girls' Mission House, in the country. It is situated about two miles from Zanzibar, and is quite surrounded by plantations of orange, lemon, cocoa-nut, mango, and other fruit trees. In the distance the house looks much like an English villa, and stands on a rising ground overlooking the sea. In front is a nice lawn. Along two sides of the house runs a beautiful verandah, projecting about twelve feet from the walls, and which forms a delightful shade from the sun. The floor of the verandah is raised about three feet from the level of the garden, and is of plaster, like the old bedroom floors in some parts of England, and like all the floors here, both upstairs and down. The house is a large one, and contains, I think, seventeen spacious rooms.

"Miss Pakeman has at present fourteen girls under her training. These girls have all, like the boys at Zanzibar, once been slaves, brought from the interior, and, like them, are of various races. One by one they have been presented by the British cruisers who rescued them, to the Bishop of Zanzibar, to be cared for.

"I hear, by-the-bye, that the girls are being trained to make good wives for the boys when the proper time has arrived. The eldest are not more than sixteen years of age, but several of the boys are older. These girls, at the mission, are taught to read and write, both in English and Sawahili, and are also taught to sew, wash, cook, and clean the house. I was very much pleased indeed, by their ready obedience and orderly manners during our stay. They sleep in two large rooms, in which the only furniture is the row of mats on which they sleep, and in which they can, if they like, wrap themselves. In the bathroom are a number of stone wash tubs fixed to the wall, and in which the girls wash their clothes.

"The cost of the maintenance of each of these girls does not exceed six pounds a year, and this expense is borne by a number of ladies in England, who each stands as 'godmother' to one of the girls, and who supply their far away children with a name. One of the girls shewed me a pretty work-box, and some other things her godmother in England had sent her, of which she was very proud. The boys are maintained in the same way, and reports are sent to England from time to time respecting their conduct. In this way a large amount of interest is kept up in the mission, and the cost is met with comparative ease.

"During our stay at the Shamba we had some very pleasant rambles through the park-like plantations, stretching for miles away into the interior of the island. The scenery here is truly delightful. The foliage of many of the trees is very dense, and of a rich green, while the grass underneath is so fine that it often reminds me of Bradgate Park at home. We usually carried our butterfly-net with us, and got some fine specimens. Some of these are just like ours at home; as for instance, the common white ones, the yellow, and a small brown one. I gathered some beautiful wild flowers, but before I got home they had withered.

SLAVES RESCUED BY A BRITISH CRUISER. (ENGLISH SAILORS IN THE BACKGROUND.)

"We had some charming strolls along the beach, which is rich in pretty shells, and, when the tide was out, we could pick our way for a long distance over the coral reefs, finding something to admire at every step. Here I saw the loveliest little aquariums, enclosed within coral walls, and containing dozens of varieties of sea weed, tiny fishes, and shells, in the clearest water, and beautifully arranged by nature's own hand.

"The breezes were so fresh and cool that we seldom returned to the house before noon, and then, towards evening, we turned out again. After sunset we went up on to the flat roof of the house, and there the scene by moonlight was truly magnificent, the towering palm trees giving a fine finishing touch to the picture. Very frequently we heard the 'tum, tum, tum,' of the native drummer, who was playing at a festival some distance away; and this unmusical noise, accompanied by dancing, was sometimes kept up during the whole of the night.

"The greatest drawback to the beautiful situation of this house is its loneliness, which is a great temptation to thieves, who pay it constant visits; and they, being so nearly of the colour of the darkness in which they come, are difficult to catch. A few days ago they broke into the house by night, bending the thick iron bars of the lower windows to gain admittance, and taking away drawers and their contents, table cloths, mats, etc. These things they carried to the summer house in the garden and then made a selection, leaving behind them the drawers and everything they did not consider 'suitable.' During our visit a chair was snatched up and carried off from the verandah in broad daylight, and this just after one of us had left it for a few minutes. The garden is also constantly being robbed. The gardener caught a thief one day, and brought him up to us for sentence. The miserable looking wretch was ready to go down on his knees and beg pardon, but at the same time defended himself by a lie, saying that the British Consul had given him leave. The gardener marched him off to the Bishop two miles away; and, as a punishment, he was brought back and made to work in the garden for the remainder of the day. It is no punishment to put thieves into prison, for the prosecutor has always to pay for the prisoner's maintenance during the time.

"We went to Miss Pakeman's on Wednesday, and returned to Zanzibar on Saturday. On this the last day of our visit, Miss Pakeman got up a pic-nic for the girls, and also sent to invite Mr. Yates to come over and spend the day. He came on the back of Jerry (the donkey) at 8 a m., and during the day Miss Pakeman and I rode Jerry in turn. The girls carried the stores of provisions, fruit, crockery, kettle, etc., in baskets on their heads. We wandered along for about three or four miles, and then fixed on a spot near the sea shore and close by an Arab gentleman's residence, where we borrowed a mat eight or ten feet square to spread on the ground. The provisions were spread on the centre of the mat, and we sat around. In the gentleman's garden were luxuriant orange trees, and quantities of the yellow fruit lay neglected on the ground. When we sat down to lunch one of the girls was found to be missing, and on making inquiry it was found that she had hidden herself away at home, having in a fit of passion vowed that she would not come, because that morning she had been scolded for some neglect of duty. This caused some uneasiness and vexation to Miss Pakeman who had not heard of it before; and the poor girl was, for the time, 'prisoner at home.' For lunch we had cold fowl, tongue, beef, mango pie, custard pudding, oranges, bananas, and dates. The dates are brought from Arabia, and are the same as are sold in England. We had some pleasant walks afterwards, only wishing some of our English friends could have been with us to see how we can manage a pic-nic in East Africa. As a drink we had the sweet milk of a young cocoa-nut called 'Madafu,' before the nutty part has begun to form; each nut containing as much liquor as would fill two tumbler glasses, and selling for a pic.

"We returned home about sundown. The donkeys here are first rate animals: they want neither whip nor spur. The greatest difficulty I found with Jerry was to get him to stop, as I kept getting too far ahead. On looking round the scene was very pretty, all the girls being dressed in white frocks with a scarlet sash round the waist, and a Turkey-red cotton handkerchief over their heads, and walking ' by one, by two, by three,' as it happened. On our way we met Mr. Pennell and the boys, who were also out for a walk.

"When we reached home the day's enjoyment was made perfect by our finding a packet of letters and newspapers from the 'fatherland.' We sat in the open air and read these letters until the daylight was quite gone, when in we rushed to get a light and finish them, devouring every word as a man would his dinner who had fasted for a week. In the light of the full moon and with happy hearts we returned to Zanzibar."

"June 24th.— We are still at Zanzibar. Our stay here for nearly a month has been very pleasant, but it has been entirely a matter of necessity, no opportunity being yet available for the removal of ourselves and luggage to Mombas. Most of the larger boats left during the early part of the monsoon, when the winds were more favourable than they are at present, and only small craft have been plying lately.

"There have been several foreign vessels in the harbour during the last few days, and amongst them the " Annie Banfield.' The captain of this vessel is a kind-hearted fellow, named Edwards. He was much interested in us, and promised to give me anything he had on board his ship. He has sent me two tins of essence of beef, three baking powders, six sardines, and some tins of ox-tail and hare soup. These will be a great treasure in case of sickness, for though I have hitherto had good health I must expect the seasoning fever before very long."

"July 5th.—A few days ago a fine opportunity offered for our getting off to Mombas. Monsieur C——, a Frenchman, had chartered a dhow for a trip up the coast, and offered to take us all free, with our baggage. She was to sail on July 1st. At the last moment the Sultan filled the ship with a hundred Arab soldiers, and we were doomed to disappointment. Mr. Yates, however, offered to go on first in her, leaving us and the luggage to follow by the next opportunity. The vessel sailed yesterday."

"July 17th.—About the time Mr. Yates left I was laid prostrate by my first attack of fever and kept my bed for a week, so I am now in a very weak state. What is still less agreeable I am now left quite alone, my husband and Dado having left yesterday for Mombas.

"Dado's health seems to have improved by a return to his native clime, and I believe he thoroughly enjoyed his stay at Zanzibar, and the companionship of the boys of the Mission School, forty-seven of whom are under the training of Bishop Tozer and his assistants. I was delighted with the order and regularity characterizing the arrangements of the school and establishment generally. The boys belong to a great variety of races, and have been captured at different times by British cruisers from Arab vessels, which were bringing them to the slave market here for sale.

"At present there are in Zanzibar only nine European ladies, *viz.*, four English, one Scotch, two American, one French, and one German, to all of whom I have been introduced, and at the homes of most of whom I have visited. The dinner parties given here are very stylish, and there is a good deal of gossip following them, as in all small circles where news is scarce. I think there are about thirty European gentlemen here, but not half-a-dozen of them are English. They are all very kind in their welcome to new arrivals, and take an early opportunity of presenting them to others.

"I did not altogether like being left here in this way, but it was necessary for Mr. Wakefield to proceed to the station by the very first opportunity; and in the meantime I have accepted the very kind invitation of Dr. and Mrs. Kirk to make my home with them till my husband returns, which he will do as soon as possible. I think I shall soon get up my strength again, as I am told people soon do so when the fever is gone.

"Every few minutes I am almost distracted by the deafening noise made by a troop of slaves who keep passing by, carrying burdens on their heads. They always sing at their work. The leader yells out a word or two, and then all the rest burst off with a sudden crash or roar, with a few words of chorus, and this monotony they carry on for the whole day.

"These slaves, like the rest of the natives, observe the Mahommedan Sabbath. There are a great many mosques in the town, to which they go to say their prayers; and if I happen to be awake about half-past four in the morning I hear, in various directions, voices from the roofs of these mosques, calling on the people to come to the services. I have often lain and listened with much pleasure to the echoing call, while all else was still. They cry out in Arabic, 'God is great,' 'God is good, come and worship Him and receive His blessing.' 'Mahomet is His prophet,' etc. Their devotion is rather pleasing, but on inquiring into the character of these persons' lives the illusion vanishes. They are guilty of every crime. Deception and theft are practised by them at every opportunity, and for these crimes there is no redress. Indeed it is not looked upon as a crime to steal, and the only protection you have for your property is to keep it under lock and key, and to be continually watching and counting your possessions. When I came in here last night, Dr. Kirk told me to be sure and not leave anything about my room, or it would be stolen by their own servants. Mrs. Kirk missed a valuable ring only a short time back, and one of the servants stole, by degrees, her whole stock of needles, and sold them for three half-pence a packet. Of course she did not find this out for some time. The same thief would also take her needle off her work whenever she laid it down, and so save them up until he had sufficient to sell. Dr. C—— had no less than thirty-three pairs of trousers stolen from him by his servants, and a great many things besides. If these religious Mahommedans see a piece of cloth or calico lying about, they will coolly cut or tear off as much as they require, and when inquiry is made, they look as innocent as a sleeping infant, and declare they know nothing about it. It is of no use changing servants, for they are all alike. The goods they cannot wear they find ready sale for in some of those dark, cave-like stores I have already described. We have already suffered from thieves. Two of our sitting-room chairs have been carried off from amongst our luggage when it was lying on the mission premises, and there is no remedy. This to me is a most miserable state of things. Mr. Wakefield says they will steal just the same at Ribé if they get the opportunity, but they have not such ready means of disposing of stolen goods there as at Zanzibar.

"Just before Mr. Wakefield left, he took me to see the slave market here. It is held every evening, from five to six o'clock. I could scarcely believe my own eyes as we threaded our way among the crowds of the buyers and sellers of human flesh and blood. The poor creatures offered for sale stood in rows here and there; and were marked on the forehead by a daub of yellow paint, to distinguish them. They were of all ages, from two years and upward; ay, and less than that, for a mother with a baby in her arms or strapped at her back, gipsy fashion, were frequently offered in one lot. Several auctioneers were busy pushing their way among the crowd, dragging by the wrist the wretched victim they were selling, and shouting at the top of their voice the highest bid that had yet been reached, while the buyers felt the arms of the poor slave as she was hurried past them. The sight of this made my heart ache, and I could hardly bear it. I had *read* of slave markets before, but never thought that I should myself be a witness of the horrid doings and painful sights of these still existing places of traffic. I cannot write the half

SLAVE MARKET, ZANZIBAR (NOW CLOSED).

of what I saw; my blood chills as I think of the look of sullen sadness that sat on the countenances of these poor creatures, and of the brutal conduct of the guilty traders in human bodies and souls. I saw many little boys like those in our infant classes at home, offered for sale that day at ten dollars each. At the same time, I felt proud of my English blood: for, on asking my husband how it was they did not offer their goods to us as they did to every one else who passed by, he said, 'Oh, they all knew we were English, and as such, hated the traffic altogether.' I praised God from my heart that

'I was not born a little slave
To labour in the sun,'

and thought how little those who often sing that hymn in our Sabbath schools at home know of the real miseries of slavery.

"The large boats or 'dhows,' that bring in cargoes of these slaves to the market, may often be seen coming into harbour, past the front of the Mission House, on their way to the Customs to pay the required tribute of so much per head, which brings in a large sum per year to the Sultan. If any of the slaves on board are sick and not likely to recover, they are thrown overboard. This act has been witnessed more than once by residents in the Church Mission House, who, on one occasion, rescued a poor woman who had been thus treated, and was washed up by the tide. They carefully nursed her, but she died in a few days."

"July 27th.—Almost immediately after my husband left me to go to Ribé, I was again prostrated by fever, and for nearly a week had to keep my bed. I got very much excited in my dreams during my illness; but by the kind attention of Doctors Kirk and Christie, and Mrs. Kirk's kind nursing, I began slowly to rally. After this I felt better even than I had been before, and was rejoicing in restored health, when I took cold, and the fever has again returned. I am now in bed, but I am thankful to say much better.

"I have just been looking through my Sawahili exercise-book to find the native word for window; for yesterday I could not, with all my vociferations in English, get our boy to shut the window when I was shivering with cold. He would bring me everything that lay near it. At last, wearied out, I told him 'Bass! bass!' (Enough! enough!) when he retired. Then, later in the day I called him back, and on his leaving the room desired him to 'leave the door open,' the simplest thing in the world. 'Yes,' said he, and shut it behind him. I called him back, and repeated my wish, 'Leave the door open.' 'Yes, mam,' he said, and shut it again. I had, of course, to submit, being too weak to wait upon myself.

"I was kept awake nearly the whole of the other night by the shouting, drumming, and tin-kettle beating of a number of natives who had congregated together in some parts of the town. On inquiring next morning the reason of all this noise, I found there had been an eclipse of the moon, which the natives regarded as an attempt of the devil to put out its light, and so they had made all this hub-bub to frighten him away, and had, of course, in due time, apparently succeeded."

"August 18th.—Yesterday, to my great joy, my husband returned from Ribé. He found the mission in a very gratifying condition. The first baptismal service was held while he was there: twenty-one persons received this ordinance, five of whom were children. The Galla women living about the station are very anxious for me to go as soon as possible to take up my residence among them. I hope my health will soon be fully restored to me.

"To-morrow is my birthday, when we commence housekeeping for the first time in 'Bishop's cottage,' a small two-roomed dwelling, where we expect to remain until I am able to go on to the station. Our furniture is mostly gone up to Ribé, but we have a few chairs here, and must extemporize some tables with old boxes fixed against the wall, or borrow some from our neighbours. As a servant, we expect one of our 'boys' from the station—one whom my husband baptized on his recent visit.

"We have again suffered from thieves. While we were at the Mission House my oak chest was left open for a day, owing to the catch of the lock having been broken on the way out, and during this time the greater part of my linen sheets were stolen, two white table cloths, and the only coloured table cloth I had. I have offered five dollars reward for their recovery, but have little hope of seeing them again. This is very annoying."

"August 19th. (From a letter to Mrs. H——.)— "The arrival of the 'Millbank' on the 2nd of August caused no small stir in Zanzibar, bringing as she did so large an addition to the European population here. Besides the Consul, Mr. Churchill, and his family, there were a Mr. Hancock, a Church of England Missionary; a Miss Rowdon, for the Girls' Mission School; and a young Scotch gentleman, who came out as a merchant's clerk. I should like to spend a few days with you in your happy home by the sea. It would do me ever so much more good than taking quinine 'three times a day.' Oh dear! this East African fever makes sad work with me now and then. I am just now recovering from my third attack, which has shaved me down thinner than ever. I don't know that having a thin, pale face, and very white hands, is a matter to be mourned over, but it is the excessive weakness which follows the fever that is so trying. Do you think I ought to begin taking wine? People are always recommending it, but I confess my faith in its power to strengthen and build up is but little, and yet I wish to do what is right and best. Fever and the wretched accommodation offered by the native boats have prevented my leaving Zanzibar hitherto. Indeed the doctor has forbidden my going at present.

"When the 'Millbank' came in I left my rooms in the Consulate to make room for the new comers, and Bishop Tozer kindly placed at my disposal a room in a little empty cottage belonging to the Mission. My husband was away at Ribé, and here, with a strange feeling of desolation and loneliness, I spent the first night in a house all by myself, spending the days as usual at Dr. Kirk's until Mr. Wakefield's return, which occured the day before yesterday. Now, having secured a little house for ourselves, and got our two little rooms whitewashed and native mats spread on the floor, and, arranged in the best manner possible two chairs, a round deal table, a few plates, a teapot, two cups and saucers, and sundry articles by no means 'too numerous to mention,' we this day celebrate my twenty-sixth birthday by commencing housekeeping!!

"And what do you think we are to have for dinner? that is, if the cooking over a fire made between three stones goes on all right? Why, roast beef and Mrs. H——'s plum pudding. Three cheers for the latter, and may she who made it live to make a great many more! Would that you could pop in and enjoy it with us. Good-bye."

"October 6th.—Of late we have been getting along in a quiet sort of way in our Zanzibar home, with our big, raw, fierce-looking black 'boy' for a servant. He cooks for us in a little hovel in the yard, over a wood fire made between three stones. Of course, we can't do any *baking*, and flour is dear besides. We get rice now, very, very good, and very cheap. We get a little bread sometimes. It is made in small puffy cakes, which are sold for fivepence each. Meat is cheap, but on the whole we find living here very expensive. We often *talk* about Devonshire cream. We consider that it incites to biliousness. Pastry is conspicuous by its absence. No fat or dripping is to be had from the lean cows, and butter imported in sealed tins is exceedingly dear.

"Since Mr. Wakefield's return to Zanzibar, he has been almost every day to a learned Sawahili who has agreed to assist him in translating 'More about Jesus' into Kisuahili for the boys and girls of the Mission school at Ribé, and with this and writing, and carpentering, and nursing me, his time has been fully taken up.

"As for me, I have had far more to do than my strength would allow: I have, however, had less fever lately, and am, on the whole, much better, and I have not taken to drinking wine either. The weather has been charming of late, the thermometer generally standing at 75° in my bedroom. This is just right. The hot season is, I suppose, just coming on: the two last and the two first months in the year are, I am told, very trying to Europeans. We have, at all times, to be very careful about taking cold, which is, I find, much more readily done here than at home.

"Our negro servant is a remarkable fellow. At a side glance he looks much like a gorilla; has a sloping forehead, great broad nose, and uncommonly thick lips, which stretch right across his face. Surely he would frighten the Sunday school children at home, although he is perfectly quiet and gentle. I believe he is truly converted. He can read and write in Kinika, his native tongue, and sings with us at family worship. This in the morning, is conducted entirely in Kinika, which I do not yet understand, but I can sing the words of a printed hymn

'Whither, pilgrims, are you going?'

which, with one or two others, Mr. Wakefield has translated, as the tune is familiar. Our 'boy' thinks it a 'beautiful' hymn. He always repeats the Lord's prayer just as my husband used to give it on the Missionary platforms at home. In the evening, for my benefit, worship is conducted in *my* native tongue. Our boy sleeps (and snores too) on a mat, just outside the door, in the open air. He goes to bed every night about seven o'clock, and it is no easy task to rouse him up after that hour if his services are required.

"Death has lately visited our little colony of Europeans at Zanzibar. The Rev. Mr. Hancock, who came out in the 'Millbank' only two months ago, has just fallen a victim to sunstroke. He and the Rev. Mr. Pennell made a tour to the mainland, to visit an old mission station. Two days after their return, Mr. Hancock suddenly sank and died. I am grieved for his friends at home. He was, I think, about thirty-six years old, and unmarried. His remains were interred a week ago, wrapped in a piece of matting, after the manner of the natives and Arabs here."

On the 7th of October, 1870, Mr. and Mrs. Wakefield removed to a house in Melindi, a purely Mahommedan quarter of Zanzibar, where, on the 16th of the same month, their first child Helena Rebecca, familiarly known as " Nellie," was born. It was not until the beginning of January, 1871, that Mrs. Wakefield was deemed sufficiently strong to undertake the journey to Ribé. Some extracts from her letters written during this interval will close the present chapter.

"October 24th.—I must just write you a few lines, although I am not very strong yet. Of course Baby is *the* interesting topic just now. Tom is not a little pleased with his 'Nellie' as we call her. She has such a round plump face, a lot of dark hair, and dark eyes. I am writing with her on my knee, for I have no nurse. Girls are not usually employed in the house here. They work at housebuilding, carrying stone, lime, sand or water on their heads, and know nothing about taking care of English babies. The doctor told me that if I tried one of them, and told her to wash 'Nellie,' she would pick her up by one arm, or by an arm and a leg, and pour some water over her out of a cocoa-nut shell. This is the way they 'wash' their own children.

"Said Majid, the Sultan of Zanzibar, died about a fortnight ago. He expired at half-past eleven a m., and was interred at two in the afternoon the same day. Half-an-hour after his decease, the new Sultan was proclaimed and enthroned, and three days afterwards, rejoicing took the place of the previous wailings; for here, literally, ' the mourners go about the streets.' Hundreds of women paraded the town, some weeping and others only looking sad ; but all making a most pitiable cry. This, however, can be stopped at any moment, so their sorrow cannot be very deep. I have often seen these trains of mourners, and heard their wailings, which are commenced immediately on the intimation of the death of any wealthy native.

"All the Europeans have been with their respective consuls to congratulate the new Sultan, and I suppose their ladies will be doing the same shortly."

"December 9th, 1870.—Our little white baby is a great novelty in this part of Zanzibar—Melindi, as we are now quite away from the European part of the town, and live all amongst Arabs and Hindoos.

"I have had a great many of the Arab ladies to see me. They always come at night and step softly in without shoes, and with dark-looking silk handkerchiefs on their heads. These ladies are the wives of wealthy and important Arabs, and they always bring a number of servants (slaves) with them. Mr. Wakefield is my interpreter, and I converse with them through him. One night, however, when he was out, a messenger came to say that some ladies wished to come and see me and the baby. No less than six came, accompanied by a young Arab gentleman,—a regular swell. I could scarcely find seats for so many persons, but they were very polite, and would not allow me to rise to wait upon them. Nellie was handed round to each of them, and seemed to enjoy the fun. I was amused at the way in which the young gentleman made use of the arm chair. After sitting in it in the English style for a minute or two, he lifted his feet on to the chair, and sat with his knees touching his chin for the remainder of the time. After chattering and smiling for about twenty minutes all took their leave.

"Since then scores of Arab children have been to look at this wonderful white baby. I dare say they think her very plainly dressed, as compared with their own crimson and yellow satins, and gold ornaments. The Hindoos, however, far exceed the Arabs in this matter of ornament. Only a few days ago I went into an earthenware shop to pay for some cups and saucers, and seeing the proprietor with his baby in his arms, dressed in a yellow satin pinafore with long sleeves, I spoke to the child, and said playfully to her, 'Won't you give me one of these fine bracelets on your arm?' Her father took it off to show it to me, at the same time saying, 'I gave one hundred and fifty dollars for the two: they are real gold.' They were beautiful indeed in design, and had a clasp large enough for a lady's wrist. The child also wore a massive necklace of gold, for which one hundred and sixty-six dollars had been paid; and all this on the little daughter of an earthenware dealer.

"It is now the 'Ramathan,' or month of fasting, with the Mahommedans; and as nearly the whole of the natives here profess that religion, there is no eating going on between sunrise and sunset. They feast all night, however. At the house immediately opposite to ours, and separated from it by a street only six feet wide, live a number of Sawahili slaves; their domicile being a kind of hut, built in one corner of the housetop. Our sitting-room windows look right down on to this housetop, and we can see them sitting there in groups in the evening; and, as soon as six o'clock arrives, they commence feeding. They bring out of the hut a large pan of boiling rice-water, and commence cooling it by lifting up a ladle full about two feet high, and then pouring it out again, and this they repeat until it is cool enough to drink. Then they fetch out a large pan of rice, and commence throwing handfuls of it down their throats with wonderful rapidity, drinking a little of the rice-water now and then as an accompaniment, out of a cup made from a cocoa-nut shell. Then they partake of a dish of boiled beans, but not like any kind we have in England. Sometimes they get dried shark as a relish with their rice, and occasionally a little meat. Yesterday, as I was looking at them through the window, with Nellie in my arms, they begged me to come and eat with them. These poor slave girls are the concubines of the owner of the house, and must lead a very miserable life.

MAHOMMEDAN AT PRAYER.

"Our house here is a somewhat novel one. The sitting-room is about thirty feet long by eight feet wide—a singular proportion; but all the rooms here are long and narrow, on account of the rafters being only of a certain length. If a room be required double that width, a row of pillars has to be placed down the centre of it. There are five windows on one side of the sitting-room, and none on the other. There is a beautiful flat roof to walk on, as flat as the top of a table, but there is no balustrade or railing to keep you from falling over into the street far below. Here the air is charmingly cool and pleasant. We are nearing the hot season, but hope to reach Mombas before it comes on. If we can get there at all soon it will be a trying journey, as there is very little wind now. It will take several days, in a nasty old boat without a cabin. From the housetop we frequently watch with interest the slaves at work, spreading out to dry or gathering in the spicy cloves, and shovelling them into bags made of matting. The breezes are often perfumed with the odour of these spices, which is very pleasant. On another housetop near us hides are laid, and on another rice in the husk, and chilies and vermicelli on others. Our sitting-room windows have no glass in them. We have, however, iron bars across, and wooden shutters, which we close when it rains.

"The Mahommedans here frequently go up to the house-top to pray. The other night I saw a man come up to conduct his devotions, and it was with evident pleasure that he beheld me watching him. He had in his hand a mat which he unrolled and spread upon the floor. He then stood up and went through various postures, and then prostrated himself on the ground. First he placed his hands on his face, with his thumbs behind his ears; then lifted his hands in supplication; then knelt down, and at last lay flat upon his face. On rising up the first thing he did was to look round to see if I were still looking at him.

"Opposite the front part of our house is a large grave-yard, with tombstones, not engraved, but carved at the top, and made to serve as a wall all round the enclosure. The grass is tall and coarse, much like that in some neglected country churchyards at home. In the day time, among the goats which graze there, may often be seen Arabs and others seated on the ground reading the Koran. If you were to listen you would think it was a feeble old man with a quivering voice trying to sing. All persons, however, read in this way here. But why do they sit on the graves to read? Because it is a public place, and they do it 'to be seen of men.'

"They are called to prayers five times every day. There is a man near us who calls out from a housetop at four a.m., twelve noon, three, six, and seven p.m. I always know the hour by this man's cries. He has a tremendous voice that seems as though it would never die away. He cries (in Arabic) 'God is great.' 'God is good.' 'He is the only God, and Mahomet is His prophet.' 'Come and worship him and receive his blessing.' He has just now called out for seven o'clock prayers.

"I do not altogether like the flat roofs of these houses. The other day I discovered that, when I sent our black 'Boy' on to the housetop with Nellie, he was in the habit of sitting with her on the edge of the roof, his legs hanging over the street, and this at the height of three storeys. When my husband spoke to him about it he said he didn't think there was any danger.

"I do not keep a nurse. When I walk out with baby, our big black servant puts on a long white nightdress which I have given him, and he walks before me carrying baby, and looking like a black priest. This, however, is the usual dress of native servants, and is called a 'cansu.'

"A regiment of warriors from the mainland of Africa passing by somewhat startled me. They were making a most wild and horrible noise, and were armed with a variety of swords, spears, shields, and other warlike instruments. But what interested me most was their head-dresses, being ugly monkey skins, with a hole cut in them to fit round the face.

I shall never forget the strange impression the sight made upon me. Some of the head dresses were made of black and white ostrich feathers, rising a great height above the head; and upon these feathers great value is set even here.

"Yesterday ten or twelve slaves, fastened with a chain in a long line, passed the house, sweeping the streets as they went; and after them came a number of female slaves, all chained in the same manner, and carrying baskets in which to remove the sweepings. They were either runaways or criminals, and this was their punishment. Sometimes they have to work harder than this. A day or two ago I saw three or four women among fifty men, all walking in single file, and each carrying a large stone on her head to some house which was in building. In addition to this heavy load on their heads, each of these women carried a child at her back, slung in a cloth, and in this way they worked from morning to night. Their wages amount to about fourpence or fivepence a day, which is paid to their owners, who return them a penny or three half-pence to find themselves in food.

"There has been another death among the Europeans at Zanzibar. A fortnight ago, a young Scotch gentleman, who came out here as a clerk, took a fever which proved fatal. A fit of apoplexy at the last carried him off only half-an-hour after danger was apprehended. Poor young man! What a shock to his friends at home. He appears to have been the youngest of the family. He died at noon, and at five p.m. was buried on a little island about four miles distant, where all the Europeans who die in Zanzibar are interred. Six boats conveyed nearly all the European gentlemen in the place to his funeral."

It is very gratifying to be able to add to the foregoing information about slaves and slavery that the Zanzibar slave market no longer exists; that upon its site there now stands the handsome English Church, belonging to the Universities' Mission, and that the Sultan of Zanzibar has issued an edict abolishing the slave trade throughout his entire dominions.

CHAPTER IX.

Removal to Ribe.

IN the beginning of January, 1871, worn by the exhausting climate, weakened by successive attacks of fever, yet anxious to remove to her permanent home at Ribé, and devote herself to Missionary work, Mrs. Wakefield, accompanied by her husband and infant daughter, left Zanzibar, never to see it again.

They proceeded by sea in a native dhow to Mombasa, about a hundred and twenty miles; then for about twelve miles in a small boat, up a creek and river, and finally, overland for six miles, to the Mission station at Ribé, where, excepting for occasional changes between that place and Mombasa, Mrs. Wakefield remained till the day of her death.

Of her removal from Zanzibar to Ribé, she says, "I felt very much affected at having to leave the many kind and sincere friends I had found in Zanzibar. The voyage to Mombasa was of all miserables most miserable. I never met anything to equal it in my life, for lack of all comfort. It was wretched to the last degree. For several days I lay cramped up in a wretched place, the roof of which was far too low to allow of one's sitting upright, the boat itself pitching and tossing on the raging sea with every wave, and the most abominable stench from bilge-water arising the whole time. When, on reaching Mombasa, Nellie and I emerged from our dark cell, I was almost too weak to stand, not having tasted food for about four days.

"We were gratified to find our Mombas house open, and

ARAB DHOWS.

here we remained five days. The house stands on a low cliff over-looking the splendid harbour, which has the appearance of a beautiful lake, a mile across, and richly wooded almost to the water's edge on the opposite shore.

"On landing, I was regarded as a great curiosity by the natives, and as, accompanied by my husband, I took my first walk through the town, the whole place seemed moved at our coming. It was as though a menagerie had been passing through an English village for the first time. Hundreds of children were shouting, racing, and screaming like wild things, and making the poor innocent fowls that were strutting about the streets run and fly for their lives. Indeed, men, women, and children alike came scampering after us in one general stream, and, after staring at us for a while, some would, anticipating our route, cut the corners, and stand waiting to get another good view when we came up again.

"Nellie, however, seemed to be the chief attraction. Now and then cries of 'Let me see the baby;' 'Bring the baby here,' 'I want to see the baby,' reached us from some of the wealthy Arab or Hindoo ladies, who stood in their dark doorways. Once or twice we stopped, that they might come and look at Nellie, but we were at once shut in by a crowd of wondering gazers; all eyes being turned on the novelty in long white dress, and little pink and white bonnet. The women leaned over, and in Kisuahili, addressed baby in this fashion, 'Oh, very beautiful, yes;' 'Are you like milk?' 'Are you like sugar?' 'Are you like gold?' 'Are you like honey?' 'Are you like pearls?' and then, if Nellie happened to crow in her childish way, they burst into roars of laughter.

"During our walk, we called to see the Governor of the Fort, having, according to custom, informed him of our intended visit. His son met us most graciously at the door, and led us to the verandah, where his father was seated. Chairs being already placed for us in the open air, we sat down, and hot coffee in tiny cups placed in golden vases, followed by sweetened water, was served to us. Leaving my husband with the Governor, I was now privileged with an introduction to the Governor's wives, and also to those of his son. The room in which we found them got all its light from the doorway, and as soon as we entered a multitude of hands were at once stretched out to take and examine the first white baby the ladies had ever seen. They remarked that it had on far too many clothes, 'One garment,' they said, 'is sufficient.' Their own children wear only a coloured pinafore and a little cap, beside jewellery, with which they are heavily laden. These ladies appeared much pleased to see us, but I could only understand part of what they said, and my husband could not be admitted. They were all gaily dressed in silks and satins, with jewellery hung in their noses and ears, as well as fastened on their arms; and they were all squatted on the ground.

"On leaving the Fort, as on entering, we passed between two long lines of soldiers, who rose up and formed for the purpose. The Fort itself is an immense place, and from the sea looks quite commanding. I was again highly amused at the crowds of people who followed us through the streets. They followed us to our own door, and then, giving three vociferous hurrahs, dispersed.

"We left Mombasa for Ribé on Saturday morning, January 14th, at six a.m. We sat eight hours in an open boat under a scorching sun, and were all this time in going about twelve miles. As we neared the landing place the river became very narrow and winding, and mangrove trees about ten feet high, with thick fresh foliage, bordered it on both sides, and threw their shadows into the deep still water. In some places the river became so narrow that it became impossible to row, and then we had to be pushed forward by a pole at the stern, and kept knocking against first one bank and then the other. This was tedious work, and we got quite weary of it. Some of the women from the Station had come far down the river to meet the boat, and kept peeping through the bushes to get a sight of the new comers. At the same time they shouted 'Yambo bibi,' or 'How are you, lady?'

"At length we reached an opening among the bushes on the right bank of the river, and my husband said 'Here is the landing place.' A number of Wanika men and women, in an almost naked condition, were standing there 'waiting to get loads' to carry up to the Station, a distance of about six miles. As we stepped ashore they stood and stared at us, but neither smiled nor spoke. We walked to the top of a steep hill close by, and sat down under a tree to eat our morsel of food, for we had anticipated being at the Mission Station by this time. All we had was a small piece of dry bread and some oranges, yet as soon as we sat down, great, strong, hearty-looking fellows thronged around, and begged me to give them the only morsel of food I had. They looked wistfully at the piece, and then said one to another 'Ah, I dare say it is *sweet*.' But what was such a slice among so many. My husband took his portion and walked down the hill eating as he went, when a woman came up to him, and begged away the half of it.

"When we were ready to start for the Station, the people obstinately refused to take up the loads, or to touch a single thing, except we would promise them an exorbitant payment for their trouble. We felt this keenly, and I confess my heart sank a little, that, after we had travelled so many thousands of miles, and gone through so many trials and dangers to reach this people, they should serve us in this way. It was Saturday afternoon, however: the sun was going down; we were several miles from our destination, and our luggage was all lying on the river's bank; so hungry, and weary, we were obliged to come to terms with them. Nellie did not know what all the hubbub meant, and nobody offered to take her even for a few minutes to relieve me, though I was completely worn out. This I have since discovered results from their extreme laziness. It is a matter of principle with East

VIEW IN MOMBASA, EAST AFRICA.

Africans, never to do a scrap more work than they are compelled to do, *lest they should feel tired!*

"Expecting our arrival Mr. New had sent down to the river a chair, to which two poles were attached, and in this chair, borne on the shoulders of four men, it was intended that Nellie and I should perform the last stage of our journey; and at length I sat in this strange vehicle, and, being lifted high, was 'borne of four.' Nellie quite enjoyed the 'shake, shake,' and cried whenever the men sat down to rest, or change hands; but I was in constant fear of our being pitched over on one side or the other; for, in the first place, the bearers were some tall and some short, and in the second, the path was only wide enough for one person, and very frequently it ran in a deep rut, so that as one side of the chair was lowered for the pathway, or the other side raised to suit a hillside, I had some reason at least to fear I should be pitched out on to my head.

"Our way lay through thinly wooded forests, and over hill and dale for the whole distance. When the way was very steep, I got out of the conveyance and walked, while Mr. Wakefield carried Nellie. There was not much of interest in the scenery through which we passed, for although the hottest season was now in progress, it was the winter as regards vegetation. The trees we passed were nearly all leafless, only here and there some were budding out, as if the spring time were at hand.

"The sun went down about six o'clock, and plunged us into darkness; and this made things, in my judgment, worse than ever. At one place I had to get out and walk across the bed of a river, which was however perfectly dry by the long drought, and, what with old stumps of trees, great stones, and deep holes, I had a stumbling time of it; for, though I was led by both hands, the darkness made it impossible for a stranger to avoid sundry unpleasant knocks and collisions, tumbles and scratches. One sight however, was beautifully brought out by the darkness, and that was the prairie fires, which were burning in all their fury. The grass here grows eight or ten feet high, and when towards the end of the hot season, it is quite ripe and dry, it is set on fire, and roars and crackles across the hills and plains with great fury. It was a grand sight, as it swept on from hill to hill in long lines of light, with clouds of smoke above. Many small trees, and much undergrowth vegetation are consumed by these fires in their raging course, as well as thousands of snakes, millipeds, and other small animals and insects. We did not lose sight of these fires until we reached the path leading to our new home.

"It was about half-past eight o'clock in the evening, when we found ourselves toiling up 'Cheetham Hill,' Ribé, and as we neared the Mission premises, right glad were we to see

'A light in the window,'

and here, faint and weary, we arrived at last. Not however, until we had got close up to the verandah, which runs along the front of the house, did we discern the faces of Mr. New and Mr. Yates, who, having heard the hubbub occasioned by our approach, had come out, and were standing there to receive us.

"We were shown into the iron house, which Messrs. New and Yates were then occupying; and they kindly gave up their bed-room to us for our use, till we could get some of the furniture unpacked, and put into the stone house, which we are to occupy. I laid dear Nellie on the bed while I took off my things and got a wash, and at once she fell asleep, and did not wake till next morning.

"The next day was, of course, my first Sabbath here. I was too tired to go to the Sunday school, which begins about nine o'clock, but was ready for the preaching service an hour afterwards. All the Mission people, men, women, and children alike, go to the Sunday school, and then remain to the service. There is a short interval between the two services, at the end of which the bell is tolled for a minute or two, to call the people in to the preaching. The shed used as a school-room and preaching-house, is immediately on the right of the iron house. This school-room is a very barn-like place, with a mud floor. The door is at one end of the building, and at the opposite end is a raised platform, with some forms on it, and a desk. Seats are also placed along each side of the building, and in the centre. Looking from the platform, you have natives of the Galla country on the left side of the room, the Wanika, or people of Ribé, on the right, while the children of both tribes occupy the centre, immediately facing the speakers. There are no windows in the room, but as the lowest part of the roof is considerably above the side walls, abundance of light comes in at this place, as well as by the door.

"As I entered the room, there were seated on the platform Mr. New, Mr. Yates, and my husband, who invited me to come forward and take a seat by his side on that elevated spot. I went forward to him, and dropped down on the first seat I came to, on the left of my clerical brethren. Mr. Wakefield spoke to the people from John iii. 16, in Kinika, and Mr. New followed in Galla, on the same subject. Of course, it was all a strange jargon to me, from beginning to end; but this will not always be the case.

"After the morning service was over, and we came out of the chapel, my husband desired me to take a seat under the verandah, just by our front door, to receive the congratulations of the people as they went away to their homes. I went indoors and fetched Nellie, and then took my seat as requested, having previously committed to memory the native words of salutation. Then the folks all came round and looked at me. Some stroked my dress, and others had a fancy for feeling my curls. But 'the baby.' 'oh the baby,' I think she was 'number one.' 'Dear me, what a pretty little creature,'— 'All in white, and what a long frock on,' were among the salutations she received. And then, when Nellie looked up and smiled into their black faces, they laughed heartily.

"In the afternoon, there was a preaching service first, and school afterwards; and now, once more, I found myself in a Sunday school. Mr. Wakefield taught the Galla class, and I sat with him. They read a chapter, taking five verses each and spelling most of the words, or reading them very slowly. One of the native converts taught the alphabet class, which contained persons of all ages, from the toddling child to the woman with the baby slung at her back. Mr. New taught the Wanika, and Mr. Yates was not there.

"The school closed about half-past three o'clock; soon after which we dined, and at sunset—about six o'clock, had the usual public evening prayers in the school-room. Mr. Wakefield prayed in Kinika, Mr. New in Galla, and a verse or two of a hymn was sung at the commencement, and at the close. Such was my first Sabbath day at Ribé.

"For a week after our arrival here, we were the guests of Mr. New and Mr. Yates, during which time we were getting the stone cottage prepared for our own use, and putting into it such furniture as had been brought up from Mombasa. The first thing we unpacked was the piano, which was carefully taken from its tin-lined case, and as carefully lifted through the window, and placed in position. I then hastily unlocked it and ran my fingers along the keys, to try how it had stood its long voyage. I was delighted to find that no disaster had occurred, and that it was only slightly out of tune. I felt it good to have a tune or two once more, after such a long silence, and I expect my piano will be a great comfort to me.

"We were a long time before we could get into anything like order, for the people at the landing place did not bring up our goods at once, but carried them to their own homes, and awaited what they thought a convenient opportunity of carrying them the remainder of the distance. We had to sleep on the floor for a fortnight, because some one who had got the sides of our bedstead had not found it convenient to bring them earlier. However, they turned up at the end of that time. The upper part of my oak linen chest did not arrive,

CHEETHAM HILL AND THE MISSION PREMISES, RIBE.

however, for some time after this, and so many of the things had to lie about in confusion.

"Our house consists of but two rooms, without either closet, pantry, or kitchen.* The rooms themselves, however, are not small, as they measure eighteen feet by fifteen, and there is a passage between them. The door at one end of the passage opens on to the verandah, and at the other end leads to the bathroom. The common kitchen and the people's huts are built quite close up to our back door, so that there is no room for a yard or open enclosure, which we might have for our own private use. Two young Galla women live in a room about two yards from our back door, so that we cannot build a kitchen there for ourselves, which we much need. All the doors and windows are always open now, as it is the hot season, and we need all the breeze we can get.

"The fame of my arrival quickly spread itself far and near; and many times have I been called out into the verandah, to receive the 'salaam' of strangers, some of whom have come many miles to see what sort of beings Nellie and I were, and we have to sit and be looked at. Seldom, however, have any of the visitors left without asking me what I had brought them from England. If I had told them I had not brought them any presents, then they would ask for a piece of cloth, or a few piee.

"I have many times told these strangers, through Mr. Wakefield, that it is not the custom in England for people to ask for presents, and that it is highly improper to begin to beg as soon as you see your friends. But they only laugh and say, 'It is the *custom* here to do so.' Even the chief of this tribe, who came to pay his respects to me a while ago, did not forget the national custom. When I expressed much surprise at his conduct, he replied 'Ah, but what must a man

---

* The annexed engraving of the Mission Premises is from a photograph taken after Mrs. Wakefield's death, when the Mission House had been considerably enlarged. More recently still many new buildings have been added.

do when he's hungry,' and then, laying his hand on his naked stomach, he said it was 'quite empty!' He came again one Sabbath, and waited about for a long time, saying his wife was coming to pay her respects to me. The fact, however, was that he was prowling about to steal, and, while we were at the service, he went into one of the huts at the back, and stole seven eggs from different nests. When service was over they were found upon him, and he was charged with the theft. Most vociferously he denied having stolen them, and said that he had brought them to the station to sell to us, but finding it was the Sabbath, he had piously refrained from offering them. Mr. Abel, of Woolwich, gave me a showy crown for this man; but I am afraid it will be some time before I shall be able to give it him. Alas, his hair is grey now, and as the old hymn says,

> 'Sinners that grow old in sin,
> Are hardened in their crimes.'"

"Mombasa, March 9th, 1871.—We came down here a month ago to look after some of our luggage which we had to store away here until it could be removed to Ribé. As soon as we arrived here, however, I was seized with fever, and for a fortnight had a severe time of it. I am now recovering; and gaining a little strength every day, but it has pulled me down very much. I have for a time been too weak to sit up in a chair, or even to write a few words. But I am better now, and I am hurrying to get our remaining things ready for removing to the Station in a day or two from this time.

"I had a ride through the town the other day, and really I got quite nervous through the crowds of people who followed us.

"Nellie gets a great many invitations to visit the wealthy ladies of the place, and very often their servants are sent to fetch her for a few hours during the day. All the ladies express surprise at the number of her clothes, and say, 'Why so many?' Of course I tell them it is the custom with English people. Then they tell me 'One garment is sufficient.' They say I ought to get some little silver bracelets made for her, and ask 'Why don't you paint all round her

REV. J. REBMANN (CHURCH OF ENGLAND MISSIONARY).

eyes with black paint, and then O she *would* look beautiful?' I tell them that English people don't like dirt, and that if ever I see any upon my dear Nellie I always wash it off. Then they say 'Why don't you wear ear-rings in your ears?' 'Because I don't like them,' I reply, 'and especially such

GRAVE OF MRS. KRAPF AND CHILD, MOMBASA.

large ones as yours.' Some of these ladies have ornaments pushed through their ears quite as thick as a large reel of cotton, and the upper part of their ears is all bored with small holes. When not wearing their jewellery they put in pieces of stick through the holes to keep them open.

"During our stay at Mombasa the Rev. J. Rebmann, Church of England Missionary at Rabai, about eight miles S.W. of Ribé, has also been in Mombas, and as our houses are near each other, we have spent several evenings together, which has made it very pleasant for us. Mr. Rebmann has been at Rabai twenty-four years. Mrs. Rebmann was here with him for fourteen years, and then fell a victim to the climate. The wife of Dr. Krapf died here at Mombas. Her grave is on the opposite side of the harbour, and on a clear bright day we can see the simple white tombstone from our windows. Her infant child too is buried by her side.

"It is now between nine and ten p.m., and baby thinks it is time I went to bed and took her with me. She lies just now in a hammock in the next room, half asleep and half awake, and now and then she calls out, when I jump up, go and give her a swing or two for a minute till she is consoled, and then return to my writing. Perhaps the chirping of the rats in the rafters above disturbs her. It often keeps me awake at night. The noisy creatures pull down the mortar, which drops suddenly down on to your face as you lie in bed. There are scores and scores of these rats in this house. They run over the walls like spiders. It makes me shiver to see them. Sometimes during the night they come up on to the dressing table by my bedside, and drink the water out of my glass. I keep a stick now always at hand, ready to knock them off when I see them. One cannot help fancying they'll be in bed the next minute. Why not? For several nights they have got my pocket-handkerchiefs, and have completely destroyed them. It is not so bad as this up at Ribé, although there they have eaten some of my knitted hearthrug, and played a few pranks inside the piano.

REMOVAL TO RIBE. 127

"Mr. Wakefield has been studying the Galla language while we have been here, and has had two Galla youths in every day to instruct him. It is important he should perfect himself in this language soon, so as to be able to teach the scholars at the Station; for, if Mr. New comes over to England on a visit he will be their only teacher for the time. It appears that while access to the Galla country is at present closed, the natives themselves are finding their way to the Missionary. Some of these are persons my husband met with in his visit to the Galla land some years ago."

In the month of February, 1871, the Rev. W. Yates, in enfeebled health, left Ribé, and by medical advice returned to England, after a residence of nine months in Eastern Africa.

CHAPTER X.

Daily Life and Work.

FOR several months after her arrival and settlement among the Wanika at Ribé, Mrs. Wakefield could only engage in religious teaching through the medium of her husband as interpreter; but in clothing the women and children, in teaching the people to make their own garments, and in leading the musical part of the services, for which she had a very sweet voice, she was already being made a great blessing to the Mission.

We shall again follow her own account of her quiet daily life in this lonely East African wilderness, and at Mombasa.

"Ribé, June 28th, 1871.—The rains are just over, and this rainy season has been a very unhealthy time. The rains often made the air feel very cold, and have made us wish now and then for a nice bright fire to sit by. Everything in our rooms becomes damp with the penetrating fogs. The books on the table, and a great many other things, are repeatedly covered with mould; and our clothes get mildewed. Many of the natives, as well as ourselves, have had attacks of fever.

"When persons here are very ill and expect to die, they wish to be carried to a little stockaded village in the midst of a forest not far from our house, that they may die and be buried there, because they fancy that departed spirits make their abode there. While ignorant of the realities of a future state, they yet seem to believe that the spirit will live after the body is dead. One day Mr. Wakefield had been telling a man about the glories of heaven, and what a beautiful place it was, when all at once the man looked up and said, '*Are there any fowls in heaven?*'

"Women often come to me to beg tobacco; and when I tell them I have none, they ask for money with which to buy some. I tell them that tobacco is a very bad thing, and express much surprise that *women* should make use of it. 'Oh, they say, 'it does us good; it makes us feel nice in the head;' and finally they go away thinking I am very unkind not to oblige them.

"We are not getting so many strange visitors now as at the first; but the people are still very much amused when I show them things of English manufacture. They are much astonished to hear the piano; laying their hand on their mouth at the sound of music. A sight of the looking-glass always affords them immense merriment. We often smile at them while they are gazing at themselves. They laugh, and dance, and scream, and then look behind the glass to see if it is really themselves, or some one else looking at them; and were I not to take it away and close the window, they would stand admiring themselves all the day long.

"I had a nice white dog given to me before I left Zanzibar, but it had not been long here before a leopard came and carried it off.

"One of our converted Galla women told me that in her own country she one day went down to the river to fetch water, taking her little boy with her, when a crocodile seized the boy and dragged him out of sight, and she never saw her child any more. There are some of these crocodiles in our river here, but as yet I have not seen them.

"We feel very lonely here sometimes. From our front door we can only seen one little, low, thatched, Wanika hut, while all around is a wide waste of hills and valleys, with the sea in the far distance. What would we not give sometimes for a little cheerful European society.

K

"Our food is not quite the same as we get at home. We do not often get beef here, but buy fowls from the natives, and kill them as we want them. I suppose they don't get well fed, for they are very poor lean things, compared with English fowls. When we want beef we have to send to Mombas for it, and then perhaps we are disappointed. Meat will not keep long here, on account of the great heat of the climate.

"Our cooking is all done over a large fire made between three stones, either by frying or boiling, and as there is no chimney in the kitchen, it may be imagined what a pleasant place it is to be in while the cooking is going on. I have no female servant to assist me, but two black boys, half a score of whom would not be equal to one of our English domestic servants. The people here are excessively lazy, and act on the principle of doing as little work as they can. They appear amazed if you tell them how hard English people work, and no doubt think them very foolish for so doing. In general the women do all the laborious work, and appear to be the stronger sex; while the men think of nothing else but strolling about with their bows and arrows, or tapping palm wine, with which they intoxicate themselves; and when they lie about under the trees drunk, they are the most wretched-looking objects one can imagine.

"At this moment, my husband, Mr. New, and the boys, are in the school together. I am not of much use at present, as I don't know much of either Galla or Kinika, but I go in to assist sometimes, and take a class when Mr. New is away.

"Mr. New is thinking of starting on a ten days' march into the interior shortly, to Teita, and Chagga, to see if there is an opening for a Mission there. During his absence, I shall have to go into school every day.

"I have a class of Galla women, whom I have been teaching to sew; and they have now all made themselves a long garment of calico, with a band round the waist, which is much

DAILY LIFE AND WORK. 131

better than the loose cloth they used to wear, which was very insufficient for them.

"Though this climate is excessively warm, compared with England, yet I get over this difficulty tolerably well. In the first place, if I want to walk out I do it in the early morning, or just before sunset, when the air is tolerably cool and pleasant. Then secondly, our house is roofed with a kind of thatch made of dry palm leaves, through which the sun finds it very difficult to penetrate. Then again, the roof projects over considerably beyond the walls, and, supported by pillars, forms a very cool and pleasant verandah, where we can sit and work or read, and where the breezes that come over from the sea are very pleasant.

"A few days ago I was sitting with my sewing just outside the door, under the verandah, when I had occasion to get up and go into the house. Almost immediately I heard a scuffling and an excited conversation going on outside. Mr. Wakefield went to see what was the matter, and found some of the Gallas trying with a spear and sticks to kill a green snake, which had found its way to the chair from which I had just risen. They seemed, however, very much afraid of coming too near the reptile, so my husband rushed in and fetched a stout stick, and soon the snake was killed and thrown away for some eagle to pick up and devour.

"We are very much annoyed by hawks carrying off our fowls. These birds of prey dart down very suddenly from a great height; and, seizing a choice fowl in their claws, carry him away before we have time to bring a gun and prevent it. Two of these large birds, however, have been shot since I came here, and measured five feet across the wings. They had stolen nine of our fowls in about three weeks, and I have lost many more in the same way. Some of these great birds are able to carry off a small goat in their claws. I have even heard of little children having been carried off in this way, but I think they must have been carelessly exposed or neglected.

"I have had to leave off writing, to go and make the pudding. 'What kind of a pudding was it I wonder?' says somebody. Well, it was a real 'roly-poly' pudding. No English jam, however, was at hand; so dates and treacle mixed together had to serve instead. The 'treacle' is a very thin, sweet syrup, obtained from the cocoa-nut tree. Some one says, 'I don't think I should like that.' Perhaps not; but we have learned to like many things here that we should not care for at home. Our chief vegetable is the cassava root, which is very commonly used by the natives. It has not so much taste as the English potato; is much harder, and shaped like the carrot. Sometimes we cannot get vegetables at all. Then we eat rice with our meat, or a thick kind of porridge made of ground corn. I have just found out, however, that a kind of vegetable marrow is grown here, a man having brought one to the house for sale.

("A boy has just been in to say that a hawk has now carried off another large fowl, and that another bird of prey is hovering in the air, watching *his* opportunity.)

"We get no English vegetables here, although we brought out a good variety of garden seeds. Some of these we sowed ourselves, and gave others to Mr. New, and others to one of the natives, who has a nice garden two miles away. Of all these seeds only one ever showed itself above ground,—a radish, and this was plucked off by a fowl; and so never came to perfection. Some small insects carried off all the other seeds for food.

"My piano is a great comfort to me, although I have not yet felt well enough to attend to the tuning of it. Sad to say the rats are constantly trying to make their nests inside it, and have already done much mischief. We have caught and killed a great many, but others continue to gnaw their way in through the cloth at the back of the instrument. These African rats are wonderfully clever at running up straight walls, and they get at everything about the place, and gnaw it to pieces. They have just destroyed in this way

HEATHEN WANIKA OF RIBE.

a new hat of mine, and one of Mr. Wakefield's, besides his best black coat, and many other garments which he can never wear again. Sometimes we have to get up in the middle of the night, and hunt them all round the room with sticks. We have traps, but the rats are shrewd enough to know what purpose they are intended to serve, and so avoid them.

"We cannot get fish here. I believe they are abundant in the river near us, but we are not clever enough to hook them.

"We have of late been much visited during the night by the wild beasts of the forest, and these leopards and jackals have killed a great many goats in the fold. A few evenings ago one came very early, in fact just after we had come in and closed the door at the twilight, and passed close under our windows, growling savagely as he went by. I was just writing a letter home, when the horrid noise almost made me jump from my seat. There is no glass in our windows, and the shutters were not closed, so there was very little to separate us from the savage beast outside. He continued pacing round and round the house all night, becoming more and more savage, for he was hungry, and the goats had all been shut up in a safe place, so that he could not get his supper as usual. At one o'clock in the morning, Mr. Wakefield got up and loaded his rifle and revolver, for, every time the leopard passed under our bed-room window, he set up a growl that kept us awake all night. Shortly before sunrise, the savage animal marched off of his own accord, and we afterwards heard him growling away in the distance. We saw his foot-prints on the soil when we walked out, but being only an evening visitor, he did not molest us then.

"We have been threatened with an attack from the warlike Masai, those bloody and cruel enemies of the poor Gallas. A people called the Wakamba have just fled before them, and, with their cattle, are now seeking refuge about a mile from our Station. God has, however, protected us hitherto, and I hope we may still be preserved from such a scourge."

"July 31st, 1871.—The chief event of interest that has occurred of late has been the preparation and departure of Mr. New for Chagga. He left Ribé on the 13th instant. He came in to say 'good bye,' and Mr. Wakefield and he prayed together, and then we accompanied him about two miles on his journey. He has taken with him ten porters, including several of the young converts, who live on the Station: so that we miss them very much from our Sabbath afternoon prayer-meetings, which have lately taken the place of the preaching service. He expects to be away for some months.

"Some of the men were unwillingly persuaded to leave, as the harvest is just at hand, and indeed is now in full operation. But I see the women have been doing double duty on the plantations, carrying home large baskets full of Indian corn upon their heads. They first strip off all the outside leaves in the field, and then having brought home the corn as described, rub off the grains with their hands, and then store it away in large rush bags, plaited like the baskets.

"The rice harvest comes next. I have walked with much pleasure through the fields, and for the first time seen the rice corn hanging gracefully like a field of oats, all ripe and ready for the ingathering. I have already bought some of the new grain, and have been engaging a woman to pound off the husk for me.

"I now go into school every day, and teach one class while my husband takes another; and one of the big boys takes the alphabet class.

"About a month ago I had an attack of fever, and was kept in bed a week; but since then I have had a long respite, and have been working hard at sewing for the people, having made nine garments last week, so that I am a good deal better. Some of these were pinafores for the little black cherubs."

"July 31st, 1871.—(To Miss M——, of Exeter.) My Dear Friend.—Do not think with many people that 'out of sight is out of mind' in every case, for here is an exception to the rule. I very often think and talk of you and all the dear Exeter friends who were so kind to me during my short residence in that far-famed city. I only wish I had the likenesses of all of them in my album. I often look with pleasure upon those I have; but the number is not complete.

"And now let me thank you for writing to me, although the two letters I have received were but short. I think those only who have left home and friends know the full value of letters. If our friends knew what beautiful things are said about them when they write to us, and how eagerly their letters are devoured, I fancy somehow we should hear a little oftener. Thank you for your promise to send me all the news in your next. I hope it will come soon.

"You may be sure that we were much delighted to receive a box from dear old England containing so many treasures, not the least of which was your own elegant present for my dear little Nellie. Thank you very much for it. Her ladyship admires it very much, for she already shows a taste for the beautiful, and bright colours catch her eye directly. She sends you her love and twenty kisses, and hopes she will see you some time. She cannot walk yet, but creeps about and climbs up against a chair, and manages to stand a little by holding on; and thinks herself very clever.

"While I am busy sewing she often sits on that hearthrug I knitted when in Exeter; and, with her toys round her, is perfectly happy, and looks the picture of health and good temper. How are the little ones at your house? I haven't forgotten them. I wonder if they would know *me* if I were to come and knock at the door some day; but then, you see, I'm too far off for that fun. Mr. New is now away on a journey into the interior, so we see only black faces from one week to another. A black boy carries the baby out, and she loves to be among the negro children when they are all at play. She knows amongst all of them the one who nurses her, and will even hold out her arms to go to him from me.

"She and I were very great curiosities when we came to Ribé at first, and, as the news of our arrival spread, people came many miles from all directions to see what they had never seen before. The Wanika wear very little clothing, in fact, men and women alike have nothing but a piece of calico wrapped round the loins. The women do all the work, while the men idle about and gossip, or get drunk. While the women are hard at work cultivating the ground they generally have a baby slung at their back, and the same when they are returning home carrying heavy loads on their heads. If their husbands are walking home with them the lazy fellows never offer to carry either the load or the child. I often feel thankful that I was born on British ground. When I tell these men that it is wrong that their wives should slave as they do they only laugh, and say 'Oh, it's the custom of the country.' Then I say, 'It's a *very bad* custom,' and they roar tremendously.

"Please accept as an apology for my not having written to you before, my long and repeated illness from fever. Everybody gets this fever who lives here; and the first attack does not exempt you from succeeding ones. Then before I have fully recovered from one I have been seized again, which has kept me in a state of continual weakness. . . . And now I must say good-bye, for the present."

"September 16th, 1871.—Mr. New has not yet returned from Chagga. He has now been away two months. He thought he might be away six months, but Mr. Wakefield thinks that his stock of cloths and beads will be exhausted long before that time, and he will then be compelled to return. The Rev. J. Rebmann has been to the same place, and the avaricious chiefs soon extorted all his property from him.

"The Rev. T. H. and Mrs. Sparshott, formerly at the

English Church Mission here, but who have been lately residing at Seychelles, have returned to Mombas. Mr. Sparshott came to see us about a fortnight ago, and we have arranged to go down to Mombas in a few days, when a little English society will be a very agreeable change to us."

"September 18th, Monday.—Yesterday began with the usual prayers at six a.m. Sunday school was held from half-past nine till eleven. Wanika service at twelve noon, and Galla service at two p.m., conducted through an interpreter, followed, at six p m., with the usual evening prayers. Buiya prays in Galla, and my husband in Kinika. Mr. Wakefield can converse in Galla, but cannot preach in it yet. All I can at present do on Sundays is to hear the Wanika class read. The boys and several women are in it. On week days I not only hear this class read, but set their copies and give them sums to do. Sometimes I take the Gallas in charge, especially when there are women present. I don't *say* a great deal to them, however, for a sufficient reason, beside the old one that 'example is better than precept.'

"The other day I was moving a box we have recently received from England, when I noticed that the side which had stood nearest the wall was all covered with a suspicious-looking sandy clay, and I knew at once what was the matter. I had the box brought out to the back door, and after scraping off the clay we found hundreds of white ants, which were cleared off and given to the fowls. Oh what mischief they had made within five or six days: they had almost eaten away one side of the box, which is now in some places almost as thin as paper. Every few days we have a piece of work of this kind to look after. The dressing-table leg has just required extensive repairs, and from the same cause. These insects also got inside one of the stands, and have eaten it hollow. To-day I see they have got into a lot of shelves, where I keep my crockery, which will be crashing down before long if I don't look after them."

"October 3rd, 1871. Mombas.—Here we are at Mombas,

in our house by the sea, with the cool fresh breezes from the harbour blowing in upon us through our prison-like windows—for we have no glass, but iron bars—and whiffing about all the loose papers that lie on the table.

"We have been here a week, and already baby and I are very much better for the change. Nellie, I think, has improved more than I have. She is made a fuss of when she is carried out in the day, and in the evening we get a good many ladies to see us. The Arab ladies are not allowed to come out in the beautiful sunlight, but have to wait for the evening darkness, in which they take their walks and pay their visits. They come professedly to see *me*, but if baby happens to be asleep they look very much disappointed, especially when they bring with them half a dozen little dark-faced children, whose sole desire is to see and touch 'the white funny thing.'

"In coming down to Mombas this time Nellie and I rode on the donkey for the first six miles, under a vertical sun, and without the shelter of either umbrella or parasol. One of the boys had picked up the umbrellas and had run on before with them, and we did not overtake him till we came to the boat landing. It was only with great difficulty, and by sending off a swift-footed man, that the donkey was overtaken, or it would have been calmly led for the whole distance without its rider. This is only a slight specimen of African thoughtlessness. The boy 'forgot' to wait for us, and there the matter ended.

"At the landing place we were gratified to find Mr. Sparshott's boat waiting for us, and himself also there in person. This was very kind. We had a very enjoyable row down the river to Mombas. When about half way, however, we drew up to the river side, and fastening the boat under the shade of the mangrove bushes, our rowers took their mid-day meal. We also opened our bags, and ate some cold plum-pudding, and drank some cold tea, and afterwards enjoyed some draughts of the sweet milk from the inside of the young cocoa-nut.

"I think we were two-and-a-half hours on the river trip altogether. The wind was against us, so we could not use the sail; and besides this, the long English oars were very awkward in the hands of the negroes, who are used to short paddles, which they dip in and out of the water very dexterously.

"On arriving at Mombas we were pressed to go and dine with Mr. and Mrs. Sparshott, as our house here was as yet empty of all comfort and full of rats and other disagreeable things. The house Mr. and Mrs. Sparshott occupy was given to Dr. Krapf many years ago, by the late Sultan of Zanzibar, and when he returned to Europe left by him to the English Church Mission. Extensive alterations are being made in it, and some glass windows from Aden, and some Venetian shutters have been put in, so that things look a little home-like. Nellie was delighted to meet Maggie Sparshott, a little white girl like herself, and she stroked and fondled her and the baby amazingly. The children are constant visitors at each other's houses, and like other children manage to teaze each other occasionally.

"On Sunday morning my husband returned to Ribé for the Sabbath, and came back here on Monday on the donkey. I was invited to attend a little service at Mr. Sparshott's on Sabbath morning at eleven, and accordingly I went. It was held in the dining-room. I found Mr. Sparshott seated at one end of the table, and his lady at the other. Each had a Bible, Prayer Book, and Hymn Book before them and three books were placed for my use at one side of the table. A passage of Scripture was read, and then the usual morning prayers were performed. We sang two hymns. There was no sermon. After service, by their kind invitation I dined with them. Mr. Rebmann was also present at dinner, but not at the service. He is very feeble and poorly, and has been out here twenty-five years, without once going home for a change. He expects to leave East Africa for England shortly.

"Yesterday we received a letter from Mr. New. A man belonging to a caravan which had just returned from Chagga, brought it. It was dated September 20th, and Mr. New was then one day's journey on his return. He says 'I have had on the whole a very pleasant journey, though it has not been unattended with annoyance and perplexity, and perhaps with danger. Of these things, however, I will give you particulars when I see you. I made two attempts to ascend Kilma Njaro; and in the second succeeded in reaching the snows of Keybo. I did this at some peril to myself and men. I have been everywhere received with a good deal of respect; but I cannot say that I have succeeded in impressing the various peoples whom I visited with anything like a desire to receive me in the capacity of a messenger of the Gospel of Jesus Christ. Ethiopia does not yet 'stretch out her hands unto God.' The country generally is in a state of siege, and the people are everywhere full of complaints regarding the Wamasai. But fancy my having experienced a white frost! and having quenched my thirst—the most severe I ever suffered—by munching *snow*: hard-frozen snow, and this in Africa! I hope to reach Ribé about the middle of October."

"He also speaks of a 'Lake Chala,' and says 'I don't think this lake is at all known to geography.'

"My husband tried his hand the other day at soling his boots with a piece of hide and some patent tacks he brought from Manchester. Before coming down from Ribé I looked into the cupboard for a pair of new boots, and found that the white ants had eaten out a large piece from the back of them. Two pairs of Mr. Wakefield's trousers have been destroyed in a similar manner by moths, which have also riddled one of my dresses and numerous other articles of clothing. This is ruinous work, and it grieves me sorely. My husband's things were kept in an iron box, and of course we thought them quite safe there. In the same box was a pretty alpaca hat, which is now quite spoiled, to say nothing of many other things.

"The other evening Mr. Sparshott invited us to have a sail with them on the bay, and we accordingly went. We intended first to visit Mrs. Krapf's grave, which is under some trees on the opposite side of the harbour, and marked by a simple white tombstone. The wind was high, and as the tide was swiftly rushing in we almost shot across the harbour, and with difficulty prevented a regular dash on the rocks of the opposite shore. We at once attempted to land; but with such a heavy surf, it became very dangerous. The sea rose high, and at last one great wave came right over us and nearly swamped the boat, and we all, with the three dear children, were drenched to the skin. So we gave up our attempt to land, and pushed off back again amid the gaze of assembled crowds, who no doubt marvelled at our folly in attempting to come ashore with such a sea; as they had previously warned us not to do so. They were no doubt amused at our wretched condition as we dragged our way home again, the glory departed from our fine outfit. It was, however, no more than my husband expected, for he was once served in this way before; only, on that occasion the boat *was* capsized, and the passengers were cast ashore by the waves. We had a very narrow escape, and this is an incident in my life that I do not wish to have repeated. Nellie did not cry at all, though she was wet to the skin and looked pitiable, as the brims of her pretty white hat hung down all flabby and loose about her face."

"Wednesday, ten p.m.—We have just come home, after having spent a pleasant day with our new friends. We intend returning to Ribé, on Saturday."

"October 11th, 1871. Ribé.—Mr. New came home yesterday, attended by about twenty men, a Mnyika of the Digo tribe, whom he found in Chagga, having returned with him.

"On their approach to the Station, they fired off their guns, and made quite a demonstration. When they got near to the house, there was such a wild screaming and shouting as

I never heard before. In fact, I felt quite frightened; for, in the midst of all, one and another would raise his gun in the air, and fire it off in any direction in which it happened to be pointing, and then go dancing and screaming about like maniacs. During this performance, they all looked the wildest set of savages I could imagine. The fine new clothes in which they had set out, were all ragged and torn; their eyes stood wide open, and so did their mouths, which showed fine rows of white teeth. The fellows danced like madmen, flashing their swords, and swinging them about in the air in a dangerous manner; at the same time making the most horrible noises; and all this before they could even come and salute their wives and families. When they did this, there was another great hubbub, of course. Such scenes cannot be described. They must be seen to be realised.

"Mr. New dined and took tea with us; and has just breakfasted with us, before starting for Mombas, to buy cloth with which to pay some of his porters.

"Our visit to Mombas did us great good; I feel so strong now, and Nellie is so much better. She will be one year old in five days.

We left Mombas on Saturday, the 6th inst. When about leaving, we said 'good bye' to the Sparshotts; and then, on looking round for our donkey, we found he had broken his halter, and was gone, and a search by two or three men proved quite fruitless. It was now noon, and we were compelled to leave. We had arranged to go by boat for the first part of the way, while the man led Neddy over-land, to the landing place, to meet us there; so that I might ride thence to the Station. At this juncture, Mr. Sparshott offered to lend us one of his donkeys, saying it would no doubt be at the landing place before us. However, when, after three hours in the hot sun, we reached the landing place, neither man nor donkey were anywhere to be seen. After waiting half-an-hour we set off on foot, and walked all the way home. The man came leading the donkey up to our house half-an-hour after our arrival. He had evidently taken his time, and now he refused to take the donkey back again, as he was, he said, 'too much ashamed of his conduct' to face Mr. Sparshott again. So we had to pay a second man to take the animal back again to its owner.

"I was very much fatigued with the journey, as the last mile or two is all up-hill; and as a result, I was plunged into a burning fever, and had to keep my bed all day on Sunday. No, not quite, I went into school in the morning, but had to leave again immediately, and pop under the blankets, for I felt almost as cold as ice. Then came fever, and then—oh! delightful, a rolling perspiration, which drenched sheets, pillows, and all, and the blankets had to be put out to dry next day. On Monday, I had fever again, and again on Tuesday, but less severely, and had I not sat up so late last night, hearing Mr. New relate some of his adventures, I should now be able to boast great things.

"I see that the white ants have eaten through and through two of my husband's travelling bags. But perhaps they may serve as sieves for riddling sand. Everything comes in useful here."

"November 7th, 1871. Mombas.—We are at Mombas again. The reason is this. Mr. Wakefield had business here, and, as the new Sultan of Zanzibar had arrived at Mombas, on a tour through his dominions, I thought Nellie and I might as well go down and pay our respects to his majesty.

"However, we were doomed to disappointment, for on our way down we met Mr. New returning to Ribé, and he told us that the Sultan had left Mombas even before he arrived there, having made a stay of two hours only, instead of twenty days, as was anticipated. This was a disappointment to the Mombas people, as great preparations had been made for his entertainment.

"On learning the news we did not turn back, but came right on, making use of the boat in which Mr. New had come up the river. It was again a very tedious journey, and darkness had set in long before we had reached our destination. I had to shelter Nellie under a warm shawl from the cold night air; she didn't like this, and being tired of river life cried to go ashore.

"A few days ago Mr. Wakefield bought a Somali knife of a man whose son slew the owner of it in battle, and then took away his sword. It is worn in a sheath and hung at the belt, and looks more fit for cutting up meat than for daily use as a means of defence. The man of whom we bought it asked my husband if he would go to the Somali country and kill the people and spoil their land. 'Why do you ask me to do this?' asked Mr. Wakefield. 'Oh,' he replied, 'because they are our enemies, and I had heard that you went to the Galla country, and ever since then it has been spoiled, and the people are scattered.' We were amused at the man's simplicity, but he was soon informed that our Mission was of a very different nature from that he had supposed. It is true that immediately after my husband's visit to Ugalani the Masai did attack the country, and this by some was attributed to his visit. As this poor man now sat at my husband's feet, looking up through his large black eyes into his face, he was told the old story of redeeming love, to which he listened with most earnest attention. Drinking palm wine is one of the greatest curses of East Africa; and Mr. Wakefield told this man that if he would *be* a Christian he must give it up. 'Ah,' he said, 'I can't do that, as I have just been elected one of the elders of the tribe, and they constantly meet to get drunk together.' I often feel very sad when I take a walk in an evening, to see nearly half the people we meet in a state of intoxication.

" During the last few days we have been out looking over various houses, with a view to remove. We really can't stay in this, as it is fast falling to pieces, and the rain streams in unhindered. Besides this, it swarms with rats, which eat up everything we happen to leave about. They run over the bed, drink Nellie's milk as it stands on the chair by the bed side, and toss over on to the floor everything they do not care for. The other day they ate the inside of two new loaves, before I had tasted them. They are not little rats, like those in England, but great slapping fellows as large as guinea pigs.

"Last night we had a very nice walk. While Mr. Wakefield had gone down to the river to take his bath, Nellie and

MOMBAS SLAVES MAKING MATS.

I amused ourselves on the grass at a distance. We heard a troop of monkeys, as if at play, among some brushwood, and making a loud screeching noise. We go back to Ribé tomorrow."

"Ribé, November 10th, 1871.—We are once more at the Station. The night before we left Mombas I was suddenly aroused out of a comfortable sleep by a sharp pain, strongly suggestive of the meeting of two rows of rat's teeth in my flesh, and springing up, I frightened off the ugly creature. He soon sprang off the bed, and darted away into the sitting-room, and we saw him no more.

We are not without annoyances, however, at Ribé. A week before we went down to Mombas, we were attacked in the night by thousands of black ants, who, in proper rank and file, made their way through our back door into the bedroom as we lay asleep. Nellie woke up about half-past four, and Mr. Wakefield was feeling for the matches to get a light, when he found the box covered with large black ants, whose sting is dreadful. Having lighted a candle, we discovered the true state of matters. Long dark lines of the enemy, from one to two inches wide, covered the floor in all directions, while other black masses were creeping over the furniture, to say nothing of the scouts, who were everywhere, so that my husband could not find a free place to set his foot. A line of 'soldiers' was marching up the side of some shelves, close to our bed, and Nellie and I were in danger of an attack at any moment. Mr. Wakefield, having partly dressed himself, bade me to tuck well in the mosquito curtains all round, while he rushed out to raise an alarm. He woke up the school boys, and the darkness was soon dispelled by flaming firebrands, which were dashed upon the floor to destroy or drive away the invaders. Thousands were slain, and the remaining legions of the immense army were completely routed, and by fifty different ways beat a hasty retreat. The only danger was setting the bed on fire, as the flames of the firebrands on the floor rose half a yard high. The next night we were again attacked, but again the firebrands proved victorious, not however before Nellie had been dreadfully stung. It was two days afterwards before the battle finally ended. At the end of this time, the enemy's now much-weakened forces were withdrawn.

"Another little incident of jungle life took place while Mr. New was away at Chagga. We had just shut the door one night about ten o'clock, and retired to bed, when we heard the savage growl of a leopard, not a dozen yards from the house. We listened again, and the loud screeching of a fowl as if in pain, suggested, as the sound became fainter and fainter in the distance, that the leopard had found a supper. My husband at once jumped out of bed and opened the door. It was amusing to see him marching forth, with a candle in one hand and a loaded gun in the other, in the direction of the retreating leopard. Other inmates of the premises were now aroused, but the wild beast had dropped his prey and fled. We now once more closed the door and composed ourselves to sleep, when the loud screeching of the fowl once more aroused our little colony. Torches were lighted, and the secret is discovered. A fine hen that I had given to Lukas a few days before had made the mistake of laying her eggs among the long grass of the jungle, instead of in her own nest ; and there she had become an easy prey to the wild beast. The hen was found still alive, but so badly torn that death soon followed. A few nights afterwards, a boy came to borrow our crowbar to place against the door of his hut, as, on the night before, the leopard had been scratching at it and trying to get in."

CHAPTER XI.

Wilderness Experiences.

IN this chapter will be continued a relation of the common daily incidents of such an isolated life as Mrs. Wakefield and her husband were now leading. As before, the chronological order of events will be observed.

"January 3rd, 1872.—Ribé.—Since I wrote last I have had an exceedingly busy time, in preparation for Christmas. For weeks before that festive day our sitting-room was like a dressmaker's parlour, or a tailor's workshop. The women brought in long lengths of print—presents from Mr. New—and wanted dresses to be made of them; and, of course, they must have the dresses made 'in the same fashion as the Bibi's;' namely, with jacket and skirt to match, long sleeves, high in the neck, and in length of skirt almost to sweep the ground, so as to be as European looking as possible. These people are exceedingly imitative; and now they have got their fine new dresses, they quite despise the plain calico ones, such as I cut them at first. I expect they will want hats, shoes, and stockings next, for nothing but the full European dress will satisfy them. After Mr. Wakefield had left for England in 1868, Mr. New distributed among the natives a lot of old clothes; and now all these coats, trousers, hats, &c., make their appearance every Sabbath day. Some have got a pair of trousers and an old woollen shirt, the latter falling over the former by way of coat, and the laps blowing about in the breeze. Some who have not been fortunate enough to get a hat given to them, have contrived to make one of plaited leaf, or of a bit of old cloth, and this they use once a week, as a protection from the sun, although their curly heads have been baked in the sun every day for thirty years before. I am often amused at their failures in imitating Europeans, for they almost invariably leave their hats in the chapel after service is over, and have to run back for them; and often on the Sunday, when any of them come into the house for anything they forget their caps, and I have to send one of the boys after them with the forgotten ornament.

"Not long ago we had a visit from the native assistant teacher at the Rabbai English Church Mission. His name is George, and he was accompanied by his wife Priscilla, and daughter Caroline, and baby George Henry. George himself wore a white shirt with a proper front in it, and after they had left, Kiringi, our Zanzibar boy, went down to Mombasa and bought some expensive calico, and got a shirt made for himself exactly like it, front and all: and before long he will be coming to us to beg a shilling to buy food. Kiringi's wife, too, has high notions. She has just made her first dress, and having abundance of material she was content with having no less than eight widths of print in the skirt, although, before I gave her one of a number sent us from England, she wore only a loose piece of calico. As a contrast to all this a young woman was sitting with me one day at her work, making herself a plain dress which I had just cut out for her, when someone came in and said to her, 'Why, you'll be like a Musungu exactly, and you'll like that.' She replied modestly, 'Never mind being like the white man; if I am like Jesus that is better.'

"Christmas-day came at the appointed time, faithful even in Africa. On the morning of that day, Mr. Wakefield, Mr. New, the boys, and others, were all busy decorating with a profusion of evergreens the school-room and the verandah. We said our friends at home would give a good deal for such beautiful evergeens as we get here. The white walls of the Mission House, were adorned with the graceful fronds of the palm tree, and some other pretty fern-like leaves, as stiff as holly, and almost as prickly. Mr. New dined with us in a quiet way. We had a roast leg of mutton, plum-pudding, and fruit pie, with pineapples and mangoes for desert. After dinner came the feast for the people. All the Mission tables were arranged along the verandah, and forms placed on each side of them, and about half-past five o'clock the tables were laden with immense dishes and trays of boiled rice, while between the dishes were basins full of gravy and slices of meat; for two large sheep and a goat had been killed for the occasion. And now all the people assembled; husbands, wives, and children, all dressed in their very best. There were about sixty invited guests in all, and a few uninvited ones, who contrived to glide in among the rest. After singing

'Praise God from whom all blessings flow,'

all sat down, and without further ceremony commenced throwing handfuls of rice, meat, and gravy, down their throats. The native mode of eating is as follows:—First snatching a handful of boiled rice from the dish with the right hand, they roll it round and round between both, into a large pill, something like a small snowball. This they dip into the gravy dish, and a moment afterwards you lose sight of it for ever. Meanwhile the left hand has snatched up a piece of meat, and two rows of white teeth soon tear that in pieces, and it hastens after the rice pill. Here and there a spoon might be seen; Chai had one, and perhaps Dado also, but it was quite the exception. It was such a sight as I had not seen before, and I could not help laughing, and saying how amused our friends at home would be to see it; but I don't think the folks saw me laughing: they were all too busy. I should much have liked a photograph of them; but we have no apparatus at present. We had arranged for treacle and rice, as a second course, but there was 'no more room;' and now all the cry was for something to drink. So, under Mr. Wakefield's direction, I made several gallons of treacle and water, here called 'sherbet,' of which they are very fond. It is sickly stuff, and no European would drink it. When they had sufficed themselves with this liquor the service bell was rung, and Mr. Wakefield held a short Christmas service with them in the school-room, which was lighted up with Leicester candles. The remains of the feast were distributed, and all shook hands with a smiling 'Good night,' having appeared much pleased with the English fashion of spending Christmas-day. Of course Mr. Wakefield, Mr. New, and myself, thought and talked much of dear old England, and I said doubtless our friends at home were doing the same by us. The day after Christmas-day Mr. New killed one of his cows, and divided the meat among the folks, so the natives would have a second feast on Boxing-day. He gave some sugar-candy as well.

"Nellie has quite an affectionate regard for the negro children. It is amusing to see her little white arms round their necks, as she presses her sweet white face against their shining black ones, and hugs them close in a winning, loving manner. She tries to lift them up and carry them, but they are so much bigger than she, that they only laugh at her attempts, while they are pleased at her attentions.

"A few days ago, an occurence took place here which very much pained me. A fine looking Galla slave, about seventeen years of age, made his escape from Mombas, from his master, a cruel Bedouin Arab, and came up here thinking the 'Musungu' would shelter him and afford him protection. He was brought into the house by the chief of the tribe, who accidentally met with him as he was enquiring his way to the 'white man's.' His reason for running away was, that he had heard that he was to be sold away to Zanzibar. The thought of this was, he said, 'like death to him,' for he would be still further away from his friends, and never be likely to see his own country any more; so he ran away. It appears that in company with a large number of others, he left his native village in the interior when the country was swept by the cruel Masai,

WILDERNESS EXPERIENCES. 153

and lived for a time in Giriama, a day and a half's journey from here, at which place he found employment in keeping sheep for a Mnika. One day when he was out tending sheep, another Mnika man came up to him, carried him off, and sold him to a Sawahili who was passing at the time. This man brought him down to the coast, and sold him for twenty dol-

SLAVE BROUGHT TO MOMBASA.

lars to his present master, with whom he had been living for the past three years. Such was his sad story. Mr. Wakefield told the lad how powerless he was to help him, but that he was exceedingly sorry for him, and that he might stay with us for a few days if he chose. He told the poor boy that if he had come to the Englishman's own country, the moment he touched the soil he would be free: but that here in a strange land, if his master should come to fetch him, we should have no power to prevent him being taken back again. The poor lad looked very sad. He was a fine youth, and as I sat and looked at his broad high forehead, well formed features, and large bright eyes, my heart ached to think that he was a slave. I should have liked to have stowed him away somewhere, and taken care of him. Next morning, as we feared, his pursuers came after him. There were four of them, two Arab soldiers, and two Sawahilis, each with a loaded gun over his shoulder, and a dagger at his belt. They came marching up the path and sat down to rest under the verandah. They soon told us their errand. They accused Buiya and Aba-shora, two of our people, of decoying the youth away from his master, as they saw them in Mombas on the day before the boy escaped, and that was why they had come here in search of him. On enquiring of Buiya, however, we found there was no truth whatever in their accusation, although Buiya said that it often makes him weep when he is at Mombas, to see the large number of his own people—the Gallas—who have been carried off thither, and are now the slaves of the Wasawahili. The slave hunters however, did not get their prey; for the boy, finding there was no security for him here, had started off as fast as his legs would carry him the night before, in the direction of his own country, and has never been heard of since. His pursuers, on learning this, had a consultation what was best to be done, and finally decided that it was hopeless to pursue him farther; and soon, to my inexpressible joy, they rose up and went back by the way they came.

"A few weeks ago another slave boy came here from Giriama and begged for protection, but as safety could not be guaranteed to him he too hurried away onward, without even saying 'Good-bye,' and we have not heard any more of him. His home was in the far interior, about five hundred miles distant. He was captured and taken with scores of others to Zanzibar, and sold by auction to the highest bidder. Poor boy! will he ever reach his home again?

"We are often reminded that our life in the jungle is a reality. The other day Mugomba dragged a snake to our door to show us. A Mnika had heard among the long grass the cry of some animal as if in pain. On making a search near the spot he found a huge snake coiled around the body of a young antelope, which it was strangling to death within its folds, previous to making a meal of it. The man killed the snake, and secured the game for himself. The repulsive-looking serpent measured thirteen feet in length, and was about as thick as a small stove pipe.

"One night, not long ago, I was suddenly alarmed by a noise which I can scarcely describe. It was evidently a cry of fear from some animal which made a spring at the bedroom window, as though it were pursued by some beast of prey. There was no light in the room at the time, and my husband was not awakened by the noise. I lay and listened, but as I heard nothing more I soon fell asleep again. In the morning I told Mr. Wakefield about it, and he said that when he had got up he could not understand how it was that the blind was down, and that there were two large rents in it. The natives said they had been made by an animal with sharp claws, but they could not tell the name. Of course I felt thankful that the wild beasts did not obtrude themselves into our bedroom, for we are almost obliged to keep the windows open, as the air gets so sultry.

"We have been very unfortunate with our English garden seeds, of which we brought out a good variety. Millions of tropical insects devoured them all with the exception of one mustard seed, 'which grew and became a tree' several feet high, and as thick as a walking stick, so that 'the fowls of the air did lodge in the branches of it.' But it is dead now. The ground is hard and dry, and the burning sun has scorched all the life out of this reminder of home. The sun has stripped most of the trees, and turned the hills around us to a dull brown colour. Brown, did I say? So they were a few days ago; but I am forgetting the fires which have been raging and crackling along the ground with tremendous fury, leaving behind them on the blackened waste nothing but dying embers and charred tree stumps here and there to tell the tale. It has been a grand sight to look out at night and see the blaze lighting up the sky above, and making it glow like the fire itself. Sometimes in the far distance the fires resembled the lighted street lamps of a large town—a pleasant illusion to us in this wilderness. Mr. Wakefield has been busy of late making a road round the side of a hill, instead of over the top as before. On Saturday last when the men left work, instead of bringing in their tools they hid them away in the long grass, and on Monday on coming back to their work found nothing but the iron heads left, the fires having in the mean time consumed the handles. Fortunately our wheelbarrow escaped the flames. This wheelbarrow is the only wheeled conveyance in which I have had a ride since leaving London in 1870.

"We brought a donkey hither from Zanzibar. Mr. New has one also, which he took into the Chagga country with him. A more tricky, vicious donkey than this I never heard of. It is always trying either to bite or to kick, so that it is dangerous to come into close quarters with him. Not long since he planted his two hind feet in my chest as I was driving him away from the verandah, and for a while afterwards I was afraid the affair might prove serious, for I had a great deal of internal pain, to say nothing of the shock it gave me at the time. Another affair, however, has proved more serious. Mr. New had ridden 'Ramathan' down to the landing place on his way to Mombas, and a boy was leading him back to Ribé again. The saddle happened to slip round, and Moti, the Galla boy, was putting it to rights when the donkey, being excessively irritated, turned on the boy, seized his leg, and tore a large piece of flesh off his thigh, which the lad declared he crunched up and swallowed. The boy reached home with great difficulty, and I had the task of binding up this horrible wound. He is progressing favourably, and Mr. New says 'Ramathan' must die now.

"On New Year's day Mr. Wakefield took for his text, at my suggestion, 'The Lord hath been mindful of us: He will bless us.' The services and general work of the Mission are going on much as usual. One new family of Gallas has lately come and settled on the Station. They were in a most destitute condition; but came, they said, 'to learn the book.' They all attend school every day. The wife stands six feet high, 'without her shoes' of course. She wears a leather dress, and a large quantity of thick iron wire wrapped round her arms. I gave two Galla men their first lesson in writing the other day. One boy has left the school and gone back to his heathenish customs, and a new boy has come.

"Ah! I must stop to hunt that rat which I hear scampering along the wires inside my piano, making them go 'tingle, tingle' as he goes, and so telling tales. If I don't get him out at once he will be gnawing at something, and do lots of mischief."

"February 29th, 1872.—Mr. New left Ribé yesterday for Zanzibar and England. He kindly offered to take anything home for us that we wished. He sat and conversed with us for awhile, and we gave him many messages of love for the dear ones at home. He came in and dined with us the day before yesterday, and after dinner looked over the albums with us, and we had some pleasant conversation. Mr. and Mrs. Sparshott have also returned to England; so Mr. Rebmann, like ourselves, is left quite alone."

"March 16th.—(To Mrs. H——.)—Our little Nellie is a very great treasure and comfort to us. I don't know what we should do without her little smiling face when we are feeling dull and sad at heart."

"March 17th.—I had to leave my letter yesterday and go to bed with fever, and now the messenger is waiting to carry this down to Mombas. I am sorry for this, for my heart was full, and I was to tell you of some of our trials. However, I hope they will pass away, and that we shall be spared to be a blessing to the people. My time is very much occupied, in fact I have a great deal more to do than I can find strength for, and I think that is why I get fever so often. These black boys do not know enough of European life to render me much assistance. By doing so much sewing for the boys of the school and overlooking the making of all the women's garments, my own personal sewing gets far behind, and I often get troubled about it, especially when I see my little Nellie out-growing her frocks and I am unable to make more. We have had some dreadful losses in the matter of clothing lately. The white ants, cockroaches, and moths, in spite of all precautions, have been amongst my new dresses and destroyed many pounds worth of our things. Mr. Wakefield has had two suits of clothes eaten up, besides hats, socks, vests, and woollen things of all kinds. A good strong box in my bedroom, containing my whole stock of calico, has just been attacked by white ants. They have got inside and pierced the calico through and through, so that out of about a hundred yards there are only a few yards left whole. I could have cried when I opened the box, for I had been to it only a week or two before, and all was right, and even on the outside there was no appearance of anything wrong.

"In my last I asked you for a 'Picture Book' for the bairn. She dearly loves pictures, and if she could talk would be able to tell what they are about. We have only the 'Illustrated London News' to show her at present. But now I must close with our kind love to you all."

"April 15th.—A box from England! Who shall tell the joy that thrills one's soul at such a cry out in this wilderness. It was our pleasure not only to utter such a cry, but to see the box about sunset this evening. And now the floor, chairs, tables, everything is strewn over with its wonderful contents, and we are in a state of the quintessence of delight. How I wish all the dear good people who have contributed so much to our happiness and made our hearts overflow with gratitude were here, so that we could more heartily thank them for their abundant kindness to us in our lonely far away home."

"April 16th.—In consequence of his recent appointment as interpreter to the Livingstone Expedition, Mr. New returned to Ribé on a visit. He spent two days with us, and we had a very pleasant time."

"May 8th.—There has been a terrible hurricane at Zanzibar in which all the shipping in the harbour, except one vessel, was destroyed, and many lives lost. We did not experience anything of it here, and did not hear of it for some time afterwards."

Writing a few days after its occurence Mrs. Kirk, wife of the British Consul, thus describes this storm:— "The town is a sad sight. To begin with ourselves. Our garden is completely destroyed; not a tree, not a leaf is left. The foundations of the consulate are undermined, so that we almost expect it will fall at the next high tide. Upstairs in the consulate every window in the front and on one side is blown away, the panels of the doors are completely gone, and almost every house facing the sea is in the same state. The gale began last Sunday night, and the rain blew in upon our beds, and the house leaked in every direction. On Monday morning it grew worse; all the roofs were blown away, and all the boats and dhows in the harbour were wrecked. At twelve o'clock it became calm and most people thought the danger was over. But my husband was watching the barometer, and he knew that the calm was only for a time. We little thought, however, how dreadful the second part would be. I shall never forget it. I was standing in the middle of our large room, with baby in my arms and the other children round me. Suddenly there was a roar and a crash everywhere. Windows and shutters were dashed in, our heavy round table was lifted and thrown to the other end of the room, the other tables, sofas, chairs, pictures, glass, china, books, carpets, everything was flying about us. How we escaped being killed, or how we got out of the room, I do not know. We managed to reach a small room at the back of the house, where we barricaded the doors and the windows with the furniture. Mr. Kirk went out to see if he could save anything. He could only creep on his hands and knees; he was blown down if he attempted to stand. The sea spray was rushing through the front windows like shot from a gun, and we quite expected the house to fall in. There I had to sit in the dark room, with my poor little children, listening to the fearful noise, and not knowing what might be happening to my husband outside. About midnight all was tolerably quiet, and we could look about to see what we had lost. In most of the rooms the water was two feet deep, and Mr. Kirk had to wade about to see what could be saved. All cupboards and chests of drawers had been burst open by the storm and nearly all my clothes and the children's were blown away through the windows and destroyed. One very curious thing happened. Mrs. Sparshott's little girl, two years old, was blown out of an upper window, and such was the force of the wind that it turned her over and over in the air as if playing with her, and then let her down gently on her feet *unhurt. She never even cried.* When the storm was over not a servant could be found. Our good negro-servant, Louis, who has been with me two years, is killed. It is hard times for me. I am quite worn out. We are very thankful, however, that our lives are spared; at one time we hardly thought they could be."

And now to resume Mrs. Wakefield's narrative.

"June 11th.—The chief topic of conversation with us of late has been the collapse of the Livingstone Expedition. England has been beaten hollow by young America, and Stanley has carried off the palm. We received a full account of the matter from Mr. New yesterday in a letter just before his departure for England."

"June 25th. -One day about a month ago, when my husband was away from home and I was sitting alone in the house engaged in sewing, a tall, fierce-looking black man, an entire stranger, came close up to the open window and stood looking right in at me. He had a leopard skin over his shoulders, and wore an ugly monkey-skin headdress. He had also hung round about him, a number of tails of various animals, while across his back were slung several gourds, covered with small pieces of skin, and a short sword hung at his side. After the usual salutations had passed between us he said, assuming an air of great importance, 'I am a doctor, and if you are suffering from any disease or pain I can cure you.' I told him at once that I wanted none of his sorcery, and that, if I needed medicine, I had it in the house. He seemed surprised at this, and asked me if I had any *poison*, as he wanted to buy some. He said he wanted that kind that if a man took it into his stomach it would kill him instantly. I asked, 'Do you want then to kill some people?' He nodded assent. I said, 'How many?' but to this question he would not reply, but begged that I would sell him some. When he found that I would not oblige him he went away. I afterwards learned that these doctors do really give poison to persons when they have been well paid to do it, and that they very readily undertake work of that kind. The natives put great faith in these 'medicine men,' as they are called; and the terrible appearance they have, makes a deep impression on the minds of the ignorant and superstitious heathen. A little wooden bead is often given as a 'medicine,' or to keep away sickness. This is not to be taken inwardly, but to be worn round the neck or ankle as a charm, as the physician may direct. Sometimes only a small square bit of wood is given, and this has to be wrapped round with twine or fibre, and worn round the neck as before described. Mr. Wakefield warned me one day against giving away my empty cotton reels, or the heathen Wanika would get them and wear them as charms to keep away the evil. So I give them to Nellie, who has a fine long string of them by this time. She is now sitting on a goat-skin on the floor playing with two little nigger boys, and a fine display they are making with Indian corn, rice, &c., in original dishes all enclosed inside the long string of cotton reels. This reminds me that one day one of the members noticed what a number of cotton reels I had emptied, and said, 'But I should think you've got a million left, haven't you?' These people have a mistaken impression as to the inexhaustible treasures of us white people, and think it is nothing for us to give them whatever they choose to ask. This false idea seems to banish to a great extent the feeling of gratitude from their minds for what we do for them. However, it is not so with all. A week or two ago I gave a Galla woman one of two pretty dresses trimmed with scarlet braid, lately received from Edinburgh. She said I was to send the lady who sent it a message 'that it was a nice dress; that she liked it very much, and that it was very, *very* good of the lady to send it for her, and she thanked her very much.'"

CHAPTER XII.

Wanika Manners and Customs.

IN the present chapter will be found some accounts of the habits and manners of the Wanika people, with whom Mrs. Wakefield was now becoming more perfectly acquainted, as well as notices of the trials and encouragements of her missionary life. Writing on June 25th, 1872, she says:—

"The other day, hearing a strange noise of native voices, I got up and looked out of the window, and saw passing down the path near our house the funeral of a little native child. It was a very different procession from what we see at home. At the head of the procession walked the gravedigger, carrying a small hoe on his shoulder with which to scratch a hole in the ground, perhaps not more than a foot deep. Behind him walked a woman with the dead baby slung at her back, in a cloth, gipsy fashion. Then came five other women in single file. They were hurrying along, making a pitiful noise, and crying aloud, 'Oh, my child, my child! oh, my child!' The poor mother, with her hands on her head, was weeping bitterly, and joining in the peculiar wailing customary here, but which I can hardly describe. That poor woman has no hope of ever seeing her little one again. To her it is gone, gone for ever!

("I have just been interrupted by two of the boys coming in to ask if fowls have a soul?)

"Some little excitement was caused here on the Sunday before last by the shooting of a large ape. Mgomba was watching in his plantation (as the people are obliged to do at this season of the year), when a number of apes came up and began to break off heads of the corn, strip off the outer leaves, and munch away at the corn just as a lot of hungry men would do. Mgomba got his gun and shot one of them dead, when all the rest ran away. It is contrary to rule here to fire a gun on the Sabbath; but perhaps he may be excused under the circumstances, for the apes will clear a large piece of ground in a very short time, and they are regarded by these poor people as their great enemies. Two strong men dragged the carcass of the ape up to the house for us to see. It was as fat as a great pig, and much more ugly. The skin was given to me, but I believe the rats have destroyed it. The heathen Wanika living near to us ate some part of the body. The meat is as red as beef, and, they think, quite as good.

"I have made some further painful discoveries in reference to slavery. I was not aware that the Wanika themselves kept slaves until the other day, when my feelings were again somewhat wrought upon by what took place. A man of some importance in the tribe came to the house and requested 'a private consultation with the Bwana.' So he was invited to come in. He seated himself on the floor with his son, and said he had got a lad that he wished to dispose of, and if Mr. Wakefield was willing to buy him, he would sell him for thirty dollars. He then rose up and fetched the boy in, and said he bought him of a Belooch, and that he kept him to tend goats; but, when he saw other boys playing, he would run and join them, leaving his goats and sheep to stray. Still, he said, he was a very handy lad, and could work well; and, if Mr. Wakefield preferred it, he would let him out to him at the rate of forty dollars a year and his food. Mr. Wakefield heard all that he had to say, and then, of course, told him that as an Englishman he could not buy human flesh and blood, but that he would be very glad to take the lad into the school and feed and clothe and teach him. 'Ah, but,' said the man, 'what good would that be to me? I gave two cows for him.' 'Well,' said my husband,

'I can't buy him, but leave him here for a few days.' 'Oh no, I can't do that,' he replied, ' he might run away; he's been trying to do so several times, and if you can't give me dollars for him I must take him away.' He was a bright, pleasant-looking lad, apparently about twelve or thirteen years of age, and had been stolen away from his home far away on the north eastern shores of Lake Nyassa. How I wished we could redeem him from his cruel master, who only half fed him; and have the pleasure of teaching him about that heaven of rest and freedom from toil and hunger and nakedness, ' where the wicked cease from troubling, and the weary are at rest.' He had on only a strip of threadbare calico round his loins, and he looked so hungry. When they got up to go away the man said, 'Have you got a chain or some fetters you could lend me, as I want to borrow them to put on the lad to prevent him from running away?' This harrowed up my feelings till the tears would come, and I will leave you to imagine us going to hunt up the desired articles, even supposing such convenient things could have been found on the premises. However, he took the lad away, and I have heard no more of him. Doubtless he will be sold to a Sawahili, and carried down to Mombas.

"There is a young Galla woman living on the station, whose name is Yayo. She is a widow. Her husband was killed by the Somali, and her little child was stolen out of the house one day when she had gone out to gather firewood, and sold for a slave. Yayo has lately found out that he was carried to Zanzibar, and now belongs to Said Barghash, the Sultan. When Mr. New was there he asked the English Consul to try to get him sent back to his mother, but we do not yet know whether the Sultan will be willing to give him up.

"We have again been very much annoyed by the visits of leopards to the station. About a week ago, as the goats were being led home a leopard sprang out of the grass upon them, killing three, sucking their blood, and then making off again. The next night he came again about ten o'clock, climbed over the door into our little yard at the back, and tried to get at the pig by scratching and pawing under the sty door. Failing to succeed here, he took off a fine hen as she sat in her warm nest with her chickens under her wings, and left the poor little things to wander about like lost children. We heard the pig grunt very loudly as we were retiring to rest, but did not then guess the cause. The next night the leopard came again still more boldly, and made a regular clearance of my fowls, carrying off no less than eight, which I had purchased only a few days before. Some one suggested that the leopard was probably a mother, and had young ones at home to provide for. However, on the following night a trap was set for her, and besides this, some of the men sat up watching to shoot her as she climbed over the door into the yard. The trap was such a one as Tofiki had seen used during Mr. New's late journey to the Chagga country, and by which a hyena was caught. A loaded rifle was fixed horizontally at about a foot from the ground, with a piece of meat tied on to the end of the muzzle. A long piece of cord was attached to the trigger, and then, as the hyena clutched the meat the gun fired itself, and the beast was shot through the head.

"This time a live fowl was tied on to the gun, as leopards will not touch a dead carcass. But the animal did not come, so we were all disappointed. However, on the night following, the trap was set again. The leopard came, ate the fowl, and through some mistake in the arrangements the gun never went off. Last night they watched again, but the leopard didn't come.

"There was another little adventure just before this, which perhaps caused a little more excitement at our usually quiet little station. One night, just before we retired to rest, Mr. Wakefield went out into the verandah, and hearing voices enquired who was there? when two of our native Christians, Kiringi and Mugomba, made their appearance with

NATIVE CHRISTIANS (GALLAS AND WANIKA) OF RIBE.

loaded guns in their hands, at the same time telling him that a stranger Galla had just entered the house of the young Galla women; and seizing Yayo by the wrist as she was at prayer had drawn out his knife. She got away from him, and rushed out to raise an alarm; when the man made off, taking with him her sheet from the bedstead, and a spoon which lay on the table. We found out who the man was. He has been to the station before. It is well known that he has killed two people, and done I know not what wickedness besides. The next day, as we were going into evening prayers, two stranger Gallas made their appearance. They came to bring news, and hastened to deliver it and be gone. They had seen the man who was here the night before, and he had told them how his wicked purpose had been frustrated, and also that he had vowed to come on the next night and kill the white man, or, failing him, the young woman Yayo. They said he was now hidden in yonder forest, pointing to a dense wood not far from us, and that his purpose was fixed. We gave the men a present for their trouble; and, after prayers, the first thing was to see that every place was made secure, and the next to load the guns so as to be in readiness. It was at first thought that watchers should be placed round the station, and if the man were seen approaching they should be allowed to fire. However, Mr. Wakefield overruled this, and each house was specially guarded on the inside only, and God took care of us all; for, when the morning came everybody was safe. The next day an armed escort, under Mr. Wakefield's generalship, went about half a day's journey to seek news of the villain's whereabouts, and, if possible, to catch him and give him a good thrashing. After reaching the place they heard that he had been there, but had left in the night for the Galla country. It appears he came to the station as he had vowed, and lay in hiding very near to the house, but hearing the guns firing during the preparations, had said to himself 'Ah, I see they know all about it and are getting ready for me, so I'd better be off.' He left the cloth and the spoon in the care of some Gallas, 'to be sent to Dunga,' but declared that he should eventually keep his vow, and watch his opportunity to fulfil it.

"Last Sunday, Kiringi, Mgomba, (Wanika,) and Buiya and Abashora, (Gallas,) made their second attempt at exhorting, with the view of their becoming local preachers.

"They tried for the first time three Sundays ago. Mgomba was the first speaker, and took for his text the story of the Prodigal Son. He spoke for about five minutes, and then went and sat down in his place again. Buiya came next. He spoke from the fifth chapter of Matthew, about the 'Blesseds.' Of course his speech was in Galla, of which I understand very little. Then came Mungoma, on the parable on the husbandman and the vineyard, in Luke. Abashora next spoke in Galla on the temptation in the wilderness, and Kiringi, the youngest, told the story of the rich man and Lazarus. I think none of them spoke more than ten minutes; but my husband thought they all erred in the same way. They told the story, or rather *read* the greater part of it, and then left it without applying the subject. Africans are not like many young beginners at home, nervous, and at a loss for words. I never anywhere heard such incessant and rapid talkers as they are. They had, however, been warned at the beginning to speak 'short and to the point.' You will perceive that all the texts of the Wanika were taken from Luke, and those of the Gallas from Matthew. These Gospels, one in each tongue, are all they have of the Word of God.

"We have had some unusually cold weather during the rainy season, which is now just over;—the thermometer at six a.m., standing as low as 68°, and oh, was not the water cold in the bath-room. I shivered like one in mid-winter as I used it, and it quite made my teeth ache to drink it. If I were in England now, I fancy I should want Lancashire fires to keep me warm. We have all had dreadful colds, and the poor natives have looked half perished in their single cloth, in the cold wind."

"Mombas, July 31st, 1872.— We are at Mombas once more. Mr. Wakefield has come down on business to see some natives, from whom to get information of Lake Victoria Nyanza and the people who live on its shores. We are often cast down at the meagre population of Ribé, when we hear of large and populous walled towns in the interior, and the people all in heathen darkness. There are some slaves in Mombas, recently arrived from this Lake; and, in a day or two, we hope to get reliable information from them."

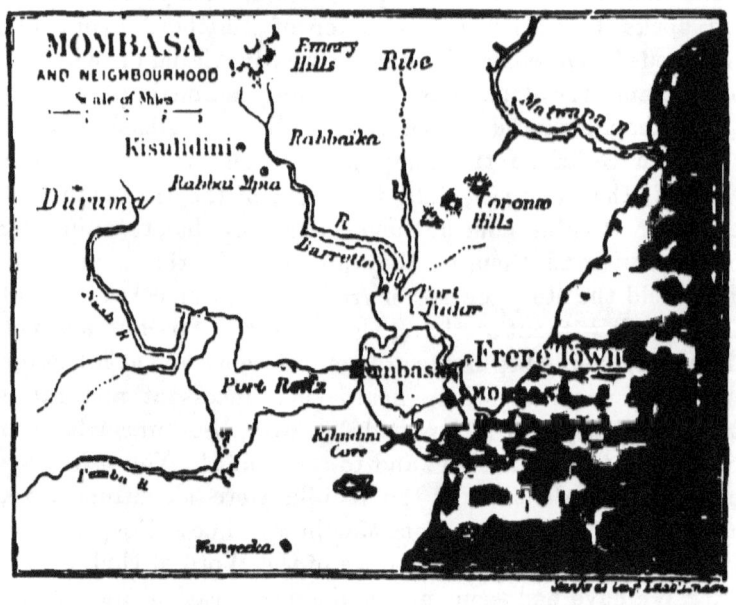

Mr. Wakefield, referring to this time, says:—"One day we had both been much discouraged at the slow progress of the Mission. My wife said, 'This Mission is not what satifies me, by any means.' She seemed very sorrowful indeed. I said that the district around the Victoria Nyanza in the far interior had sometimes been in my mind. There were populous towns on the shores of the Lake, and masses of people to work among: but the journey would be long and

MAP OF EASTERN AFRICA.

perilous, the situation more entirely isolated than even at Ribé, and the people in a most savage and depraved state. Would she be willing, I asked her, to go to the Nyanza with me if duty pointed in that direction. She looked thoughtfully on the ground for a moment: then raised her head, and firmly replied 'Yes.' I felt my heart glow with admiration for her devotion and heroism of spirit. Yes; she was willing to go anywhere for Christ."

We now return to Mrs. Wakefield's own narrative.

"Nellie and I came down here for a change of air. We have been pent up in our little two-roomed cottage at Ribé for eight months, and we hope the sea breezes will do us good.

"In coming down from Ribé, Nellie and I, as usual, rode on the donkey for the first six miles, and then we took boat for Mombas. (*See page* 170.) The boat was one hollowed out of the trunk of a single tree, and we squatted down on a rush mat in the bottom of it. Nellie was delighted to see the water and watch the paddles dipping in and out, and to see the large birds which kept flying over our heads; but we all got tired before our six hours' voyage was accomplished. The tide was against us, and this made the rowing slow and hard work, and the sun had gone down some time before we reached Mombas.

"Next morning, after I had give Nellie her bath, Mr. Wakefield called out, 'Letters from England!' But I must now clear away my writing materials, for Mr. Wakefield has to go to bed on the table. He prefers this to the floor, which is sopping wet. We caught several buckets full of water yesterday in our bed-room, and it is now drip, drip, dripping through the ceiling."

"August 1st.—To go back to the news from home. I nearly cried for joy when I saw the large parcel of newspapers, letters, magazines, etc., all for ourselves. It *was a* delightful welcome to Mombas, and made us forget all the weariness and headaches caused by the journey of the previous day. We read a letter from Mr. New first, dated Seychelles, July 3rd, in which he said that after joining with the famous Stanley, Lieut. Henn, O. Livingstone, and Captain Morgan, of the wrecked *Lobelia*, in chartering a vessel to Seychelles, they had just missed the mail for Europe by a few hours, and were therefore detained at Seychelles a whole month! However, he hoped to leave next day, and to arrive in England before the Assembly was over.

"A lot of Hindoo boys have been to me to-day, bringing an egg each, which they wanted to exchange for a picture. I gave them a leaf or two of some very old copies of the 'Illustrated London News,' with which they were much pleased, and soon I had more demands than I could supply.

"Whenever we come down to Mombas, the children come begging for toys or something to play with. Toys cannot be bought here. Nellie's dolls are very much coveted. Many grown up men at Ribé have asked me for one, that they might take it away to their far off home *to play with*."

"Ribé, October 8th, 1872.—It is now five minutes to twelve o'clock, rather late to begin writing. The fact is that, weary and worn, and thoroughly exhausted at the close of the day, and having put Nellie to bed I fell asleep, and after a long nap I was awakened by nightmare. I had been dreaming that I went to the back door to get something that was out in the yard; when I got to the door I heard a sound of the crunching of bones by some animal outside, so was afraid to venture to get what I wanted, and came into the room and sat down again. In a few minutes, however, I thought 'How foolish I am; perhaps it was only a wild dog, for it was quite dark, and I was unable to see. So I took up our little paraffin lamp, and, putting on a bold face, went towards the door again, which I had left ajar; but just as I reached it the door was pushed gently open from the outside, and to my intense horror a leopard walked gracefully in. I dashed the lamp I held in my hand in his face, smashing chimney and all into a thousand pieces, and then fell swooning back upon the floor, vainly trying, as I thought, to scream out, 'Where's Nellie? run! save the child! Nellie! Nellie!' I gave some inarticulate sound, which awoke me in a cold sweat; and immediately after, I heard Mr. Wakefield calling out 'Hey! Reb! what's the matter? come and have some tea; its nearly cold, and I want to write a letter to the Missionary Secretary to-night.' So that is the reason I am burning midnight oil. It was only a dream about that leopard, but it makes one think and dream when we have so many wild beasts round the house every night. Mgomba saw a leopard hiding in the hedge, a few yards from our door, the other morning when he went out to ring the bell for morning prayers, at six o'clock. The beast was waiting until the fowls turned out, that he might be able to carry three or four off for his breakfast. However, when he saw Mgomba, he sprang into the long grass, and went bounding away to his lair in the forest.

"A short time ago we were sitting quietly in the house one evening, when suddenly Mr. Wakefield laid down his book and I my work to listen to a hyena crunching bones in the verandah, just under the window of the room in which we were sitting. Perhaps he lay there to get the benefit of the light. A cow was killed the day before, and bones were thrown about. I should think he sat twenty minutes enjoying his supper. My husband went out at the back to call Tofiki to come and shoot him; but his gun was not loaded, so we allowed the animal to finish his meal in peace. The next night we placed some more bones and a loaded gun ready for him; but he didn't come. We opened the window a little way and peeped out once or twice into the moonlight, but we saw nothing of him. The night before one of the boys, happening to go out late, saw the huge beast, and they afterwards heard him growling near their house.

"At another time, between two and three o'clock in the morning, we heard a great noise amongst the fowls; and on going out, found all the boys out too, armed with bows and arrows, for they had heard the noise also. Presently it was discovered that an animal, called by the natives 'Cala,' was inside the fowl enclosure. They tried to shoot it, but it bolted out and made off. The cala is a small animal with a long body and very short legs; a sharp nose, and a long tail of a greyish colour. It had been carrying off fowls every night for some time; but we could never find out how it got in, and though we rushed out in the middle of the night for several nights following when roused up by the screeching of the fowls, we never saw anything, and concluded the rats had done the mischief.

"And now I mention rats I am reminded that a night or two after I last wrote to you, a rat gave my big toe such a nip as I shall not soon forget. I thought at first it was bitten right off, but I was glad to find, on examination, that it was not so, and that it was only a rat's visit; and I tried to settle off to sleep again. In about two minutes, however, he was round my pillow cutting his capers; so I thought it was time to interfere. Turning on the light, Mr. Wakefield and I got a good stick apiece, and hunted him round and round the room for about half an hour, not giving up the chase until we had killed him and thrown him out as food for the hawks. He hid away once in the little top drawer of the mahogany set, which was a little way open. When we poked him out with a stick he sprang down on to my bare feet and gave me four long scratches, which hurt me for nearly a fortnight. I do believe rats have venom in their claws, like cats. It is very difficult to catch a rat in this house, we are so crowded up with things in these two rooms.

"But, worse than rats, the white ants are always busy. About a week ago we accidentally discovered that six or eight volumes of 'Wesley's Works' were all but eaten up, although the back and sides of the books were perfectly whole. Many other smaller books that were on the same shelf were completely destroyed, as 'Mount of Olives,' a new Hymn Book, 'Life in Light,' 'The Bishop's Little Daughter' by

Bishop Tozer's sister; a Geometry Book, and several others. A large Cyclopædia, in eighteen volumes, is almost ruined.

"Nellie speaks the native language, although she understands English. Mr. Wakefield says she will soon beat me at talking Kinika. She is a dear, affectionate little thing. To-night, when I lay on the bed with neuralgia in my head and face, she climbed up and looked so pitifully at me; then kissed me, stroked me, and finally put her little face against my own and her tiny arm round my neck, and tried to hush me to sleep saying, 'Bye-by, mamma.'

"Mr. Wakefield has been very poorly too, and I have had fever hanging about me. Perhaps the change of seasons has had something to do with it. The hot season is coming upon us. Yesterday I noticed that the grass had been fired, and, from a long line of smoke heard the rush and crackling of the fire underneath it as it was tearing along. Some man who had also noticed it said it was a *sin* to burn it now that the people are all busy cutting grass for roofing their houses. Mr. Wakefield is buying a good deal of it too. He intends to use it in the future instead of makootee, which is very expensive, and wants renewing every two or three years. Makootee is made by tying the dried leaves of the cocoa-nut palm on to long sticks, thus making a sort of fringe rather more than half a yard deep. These fringes are laid on to the roof and tied, so as to overlap each other, as slates do at home, only *these* slates are nearly two yards long by nearly three quarters deep. One hundred of them costs a dollar, and there are two thousand on the station, which require to be renewed every two years.

"We are all alive just now with a native builder and carpenter at work putting up a new room at the end of this little cottage. The walls are being built of mud and stone, and men and boys are busy carrying stones down from the top of the hill, while half a dozen women, with large, round, clay vessels on their heads, are going to and from the river, half a mile distant, carrying water to supply the clay-treaders. They say it is tiring work mixing those large mud pies, for they stand nearly up to their knees in the 'mixture.' When one lot is ready they throw it out with their hands, making a large heap, from which the mason gets his supply; then get more sand and more water, and begin mixing again. All the workmen rest for two hours in the middle of the day because the sun is so hot, and men are not strong here like they are at home. I am often amused at the large number of them it takes to lift a heavy box or move a log of wood. When I tell them about one man in England carrying a sack of flour they look amazed. Then again, when they hear that in England people work every day and all the day long from morning till night to get a living, they think that it must be almost worse than slavery itself, and how men can like it they cannot imagine. Here the heathen Wanika come to work one day and then rest the next two to make up for it. It is a very rare thing to be able to engage a man to work for a month. If you do so they come to you in about a fortnight to beg off, as 'their own plantation requires their attention,' or 'they have some friends at a distance who have important business with them.' Or else at the end of the third week they 'think the time *very* long and enquire how many days remain to complete the engagement, frequently coming to say the term is up three or four days before the time. It is at such times very difficult to convince them that it is not so, although you tell them you have got the date written down, and that you go by the almanack and not by their moonshine reckoning. They go sulkily away at last, with the conviction that they are being cheated; and prefer in future to work by the day, so as to be able to come and go just when it suits them. These people have no ambition, and therefore never try to better their circumstances, but live every day from hand to mouth. A couple of yards of common calico round their loins satisfies them for clothing, and this is worn until it drops off in rags, all heavy with filth and vermin.

"The walls of our own house, when built, are plastered over with a coating of mortar made of lime, which is obtained at Mombas, and is very dear. Although the lime costs so much, and the loads for the carriers were made very small, many of the Wanika opened the bags on the way, and emptied quantities of lime amongst the long grass of the jungle, and it was a long time before they were detected. Even then the transgressors denied all knowledge of the matter, with the utmost possible coolness, as lying is considered no sin among them.

"While we were at Mombas we got news that six sheep were missing from the flock, namely, two of our own, two of Mr. New's, and two of a neighbour's. On our return home, enquiry was made in every direction, and a clue at length obtained. A man at Rabai said he knew who had taken them, but would not tell us unless he were presented with a couple of dollars and some cloth. However, he was talked down to one dollar; and, after sundry preliminary visits, he said a young man named Katamah had taken them, and had sold them for dollars. This was news worth having, for, although it is well known that there are few honest heathen men in Ribé, this Katamah we had never suspected. He came to the Station every day in his walks, and had cut a good many poles for building mud cottages here. Mr. Wakefield had also bought a great deal of makootee of him, and I knew him better than most of the other heathen Wanika. But, to make a long story short, one day when he came to the Station, my husband called Tofiki, and said, 'Here's a piece of cord; tie this man's hands, he's a thief; he has stolen my sheep.' The man submitted to the pinioning quite patiently, saying that he was as 'innocent as a lamb' about the matter, and trying to look so, too. Three or four nights' lodging in the iron house, however, brought things to his remembrance; and, having communicated with his friends, four of the sheep were brought back. The thief now begged to be released, 'that he might go and hunt the other two,'

which happened to be our own. Of course, leave was not
granted, until one day he took it himself. Once or twice
every day he was led out for a walk with a length of rope
tied to his hands, when one day, having led his keeper to a
long distance from the house, he suddenly made a spring;
the rope broke, and he rushed off like lightning into the
jungle, leaving his jailor with part of the rope in his hand.
All at once we heard a great outcry for help, and half a
dozen swift-footed men belonging to the Station started in
pursuit. But the thief was like a young hart on the moun-
tains; and, as he had a good start, defied all their attempts
to overtake him. They tracked him a long way by the trail
he left in the grass; but then, suspecting this, he grew
crafty, and took to leaping, and so they lost scent, and he hid
away in the forest. Mr. Wakefield immediately offered a
reward for his capture; but no brother Mnika would disclose
his hiding-place, as they sympathize with each other in common, and against the Moosungoo, or white man. A few days
ago, however, a deputation waited on my husband from the
elders of the tribe, to intercede for liberty for the thief to
roam at large for three months, until he could get the money
to pay for the missing sheep. The deputation brought part
of the money with them. He listened to their request, when
one of them went aside, and to our great astonishment
returned with the delinquent. He began to walk up to us;
but, when within half a dozen yards, the elders cried out to
him, '*Down on your knees! down on your knees!*' on which he
dropped down and came crawling along the verandah to Mr.
Wakefield's feet. He then confessed that he had done wrong,
but said 'the Devil had tempted him.' Whenever he lifted up
his head to speak the elders pushed it down again, and made
him hold it down till he had done speaking, when he withdrew
to a distance, and the agreement for bringing the remainder
of the money was completed. The old men now begged that
they might at once receive a share of the money for their
trouble; but my husband said, 'Wait until the matter is quite

settled,' and so they went away. I have never seen Kata-mah since; but we hear that he is hunting the cash at some distance. It is astonishing how scarce visitors to the Station have been since this affair, as these sheep are only one theft out of many committed here, and doubtless men's consciences are calling their sins to remembrance. I ought to have said that the thief who ran away had previously gnawed at the rope until it was nearly severed, and had thus succeeded in snapping it in two, and making off.

"A still more trying circumstance, and of a painful nature, as being connected with the church, took place a short time ago. One evening Buiya came in to have a talk with Mr. Wakefield. He was formerly a great man in his own country, and my husband saw him during his first visit to the Galla land. He then wore four plaits of hair about four inches long, at the back of his head, as a sign of his importance, and to show that he had, with his own hand, killed one or more men. Some time after this the Masai ravaged the country, carried off all the cattle, and left the inhabitants almost without the means of subsistence. Many of these left the country, and Buiya and his family were among the number. While Mr. Wakefield was in England Buiya came to the Station at Ribé with his wife and two children, all reduced through hunger. Mr. New took them in, and fed them for a long time. He also provided them with a house and plantation, and supplied them with everything they needed. The woman, Safo, whom Buiya brought with him, was not his real wife; he had stolen her from another man, and had lived with her for several years. At length Safo's real husband died, and Buiya declared to Mr. New, that now her husband was dead she was and ever would be his lawful wife. Buiya soon expressed a desire to 'enter the Book,' and ultimately he and his wife Safo were baptized.

"Buiya is a man of bright, cheerful countenance, and seems much more intelligent than any of the Wanika. A little before we arrived at the Station a brother of Buiya's died, and left a young widow, Harfa, about seventeen years old, who according to the Galla law, fell to Buiya as *his* wife. Buiya was, in any case, her protector, and he went and fetched her from the Galla country to live on the Station, in the same house with his mother. From the time that this young girl Harfa came to Ribé, Buiya began to be uneasy. He would come in to Mr. New and say how his fellow countrymen were continually taunting him for retaining Safo. Mr. New would tell him to take no notice of them, and then he would come in and say, in a canting way, that he had been very much troubled in his own mind about the matter, and that he was afraid that if he still kept Safo he shouldn't get to heaven. Both Mr. New and my husband had a long talk with him about it.

"At length, some time after Mr. New had left for England, it became evident that Buiya had fallen from grace, and he distinctly announced his intention to leave the Mission and to take Harfa as his wife. Mr. Wakefield expostulated with him, and reminded him of the foul sin he was about to commit, and that Satan had evidently got fast hold of him, and was bent on his destruction. But all that he said in reply was, 'I shall go, I shall go.' 'What?' said my husband, 'give up Christ? give up the Book?' 'Oh no,' he replied, 'I shall not give up Christ.' All his warnings, entreaties, and persuasions were apparently thrown away, although the interview lasted until one o'clock in the morning. Buiya remained for some days after this, during which time every effort was made to reclaim him. A meeting of the whole church was held, but Buiya's heart and face seemed like a flint. He took no heed to what was said, but after the meeting was over said, 'I shall go.' And in a few days afterwards he bade us farewell.

"This was the leading man in the church (amongst the Gallas) who had always had so much to say, and was a prayer leader and exhorter; and his fall has had a very damaging effect upon the Station. He has written to Mr.

Wakefield since he left, to say that the Governor of the coast-town, Takaungu, had told him that the religion of the white man was all lies, and bad; and had advised him to give up all the notions he had gained while at Ribé. The chief of the Galla country has also called Buiya to him, to inform him of what he has learnt here. We hear that this chief says that he believes that the reason why the Galla country has been spoiled is because of the wickedness of the people; and that he is deliberating whether it would be well for them, as a nation, to accept the teaching of the white man. It may be that thus the Lord is opening up the country for the Gospel; but whether any credit is to be placed on these reports, I cannot say.

"How exceedingly trying all these things are. I am sure a Missionary needs a great deal of wisdom to know how to deal with such cases. The Gallas are a most cunning, and yet smooth-speaking people, and their greed passes all description. They are lazy, too, like nearly all Africans, and I think they detest work with even a greater detestation than other races of Africa. Take one instance. A stranger Galla once wished to go down to Mombas, under Mr. New's protection, and to get the advantage of the boat-ride instead of walking. 'All right,' said Mr. New, 'you can go if you'll carry this small carpet bag for me down to the landing-place.' The man shook his head and refused the task, and therefore missed the opportunity of going to see his brother at Mombas, for he was afraid to go alone lest he might be seized and sold for a slave.

"The Sawahilis and Arabs are always on the look out for men, women, and boys *alone*, that they may capture and sell them. The day before yesterday, the wife of Mgomba, and the wife of Kiringi, both members of our church, and another woman, went four or five miles from the station, to buy each an earthenware cooking pot. On returning homeward, they espied two or three Sawahili men hiding behind a tree, on the watch to kidnap helpless passers by. Finding out their danger, the poor young things flung down their cooking pots from their heads, and ran for their lives, only just managing to escape the men, who, at one time, were close behind them. If they had been captured, who could have compelled their captors to restore them? What power have we with Mohammedan law ruling the country? It makes us more than ever detest that horrid system of slavery and all its abominations!

"Mr. Wakefield and I went one day to see a native funeral. We heard a great noise in the Kaya (about a mile away) one morning, as we were sitting at breakfast; and on inquiry, we learned that a youth, about seventeen years of age, had died, and was about to be buried. A man who was sitting in the verandah, said to us 'Come, and let us go and bury him!' After a little conversation we decided to go, and started, Nellie and the boys accompanying us. The Kaya is a dense forest, in the middle of which are a few huts, all fenced round, and here the people live in time of war. In this sacred enclosure all who die in the Kaya are buried, and sometimes, when people are very ill, they are hurried off to this forest, that they may die there. This youth was not buried within the enclosure, but in an open space near the path leading to it. The Wanika all wish to be buried in or near this spot, as they say the departed spirits love to hover there.

"On arriving at this place, we found a large number of women sitting under some trees; and in the centre of the group lay the corpse of the young man Munga. It was wrapped in a cloth and a piece of matting, and laid on some sticks, which were tied together so as to form a sort of bier. The women, about a hundred in number, were all wailing and crying in a most pitiful manner. A young girl, however, to whom the youth was betrothed, surpassed all the others in her piercing cries, although she appeared otherwise quite unconcerned, and was gazing around her all the time, while not a single tear fell from her eyes. She appeared to be about thirteen or fourteen years of age. At a little distance a score or two of men were dancing in a ring, with a number of jingling ornaments tied on their legs. They were keeping time to the drum by clapping their hands, as only Africans can clap, and humming a monotonous tune between. The noise was almost deafening, as it came with a 'clap, clap altogether.' Presently some women came and joined the ring, and the men danced before them so close together as to rub faces; but their arms were kept straight down by their sides. About this time, a man came up to us, and asked us to move a little further away, as a woman had been seized by the devil, and she was afraid to see us so near. Of course we did as requested; but soon the man came back with a different story. He now begged us to come up quite close to where the woman was, for they believed that if we were only to step quite near her, the devil would be so frightened that he would be sure to make off at once. I felt somewhat amused at the request, but we did not try what influence our presence might have on the possessed one. The power of casting out devils has not, I fear, been continued to the 'Apostolic succession.'

"We now went to the grave, which five or six men were engaged in digging; some scratching with hoes, and others throwing away the soil. While all was being prepared, we walked to and fro under the cool shade of the thick trees, or sat on a fallen stump watching the passers by: for the noise was too deafening for us to remain near the mourners for any length of time. The nearest relatives of the deceased boy kept walking about in front of the corpse, sobbing and wailing most piteously. About two o'clock the grave was ready. It was of unusual depth, perhaps five feet, and for four feet of the distance down it was a yard across. Below this it was only a narrow trench, just sufficiently wide to lay the body in. After the people had gone to take a last look at the face of the dead boy, the body was taken up, and the wailing began afresh. Just before starting to the grave, a live sheep was brought and laid on the ground, immediately at the feet of the corpse, killed as a sacrifice, and then thrown aside. The procession then moved on for three or four yards, when a goat was brought and killed in the same way, the blood running along the footpath. The corpse was now brought to the grave. The outside matting was taken off, and the body was wrapped in a piece of new calico besmeared with grease, and I saw it lowered into its last resting place. The body was placed on its side, in the narrow trench I have spoken of. A wooden vessel was now brought, which appeared to contain some clear-looking liquid, that the people said was 'medicine.' This was intended to be poured into the ear of the corpse, but the calico being new, the water ran off, and this, perhaps, answered quite as well. Another clean piece of calico was now spread over the body; then a number of sticks were laid across; then a piece of matting; after which the grave was filled up. Another goat was now brought to the mouth of the grave, and, while men held it down, its throat was cut, and the blood flowed into the grave. After fencing around the grave with sticks to keep away the hyenas the ceremonies were over. As we came away the men were cutting up the carcasses of the sheep and goats, to be roasted for a general feast. We were strongly pressed by the people to remain until the meat was cut up, that we might carry home a portion with us; but we thanked them for their generosity, and declined the favour.

"Mr. Wakefield has recently translated into Kinika Philip Philips' little hymn, 'Never be afraid,' and the boys have learnt the tune, and sing it right heartily. We hear them singing it all the day through, as they pass to and fro. He has also composed a hymn, 'Praying for the Holy Spirit,' which we have taught them to sing to the tune 'Rockingham.'"

CHAPTER XIII.

Visits and Visitors.

WITH this chapter will terminate Mrs. Wakefield's own lively sketches of the chequered incidents and scenes of her missionary career at Ribè and in its immediate neighbourhood.

Her life itself was now rapidly drawing to a close. Before the first half of the year 1873 had passed away the terrible illness which was to remove her at once from her work and from the world had seized her in its relentless grasp, and the hand to which the reader has owed so large a portion of this volume could write no more.

Meanwhile we will follow her as she traces the more interesting events of the last few months of her working life.

"Ribè, December 5th, 1872.—Helena's birthday, which occurred on October 16th, we kept in the best way we could. For the boys we made a feast of rice and meat, and a sweet drink made of treacle and water; gave them a holiday, and in the evening displayed the magic lantern. I cannot express how amazed and delighted they all were with the moving figures, as they had never seen anything of the kind before. When this was over Nellie presented all the boys with a nice, clean little book, into which to copy all the hymns we sing here. I made the books, sewing them together, and then pasting on covers made from some choice patterns of wallpaper which we brought out with us. The books looked quite dashing, and the boys were evidently much pleased.

Since then I have been ruling the books, and teaching the boys to copy the hymns neatly into them. We sing about twenty hymns in the native tongue. For one new boy, who cannot yet write much, but with whom I have been taking much pains to teach to read, I have made a hymn book, copying in all the hymns in printed characters, which has cost me no little time. But about Nellie's birthday. I had made a large plum-pudding for dinner, and as we ate only a small piece of it, Nellie handed the rest on a plate to the boys that they might all have a taste. Then she gave them a kiss all round, and they all wished her good night and 'many happy returns of the day;' or, as they put it, that she might 'live all the days,' or that she might 'live for ever.'

"It is evening now. We have had some tropical flooding rain, which has cleared the atmosphere, and now I am feeling somewhat better. While I am writing I hear the boys, as they sit outside near the door of their house in the moonlight, singing one of the new hymns to the tune 'Rockingham,' which they like very much; and it sounds quite homelike, although perhaps their voices, as a whole, are not quite as harmonious as those of better trained scholars in England. They keep very good *time*, however, and that is more than can be said of all singers.

"One thing that takes up a deal of time in the mornings, just after breakfast, is the dispensing of medicines and advice to invalids. Not merely is medicine given to the sick *on the Station*, but strangers come from all parts to be treated, making journeys of twenty, thirty, and forty miles, and even farther, trudging all the way on foot. A poor old woman, whose home is forty miles away, came some time since, and is still here taking medicine three times a day, for what I think is deep-seated consumption. She has a fearful cough, and her body is very much wasted. Another patient who is staying here, and for whom I have made linseed poultices every day for months, comes from a place thirty miles distant, with large wounds of six years standing on his hands and legs, and hopes by and by to leave here perfectly cured. He has tried many remedies, among others conversion to Mohammedanism, but all have hitherto failed. Kamnazo, the boy whom I have been teaching to read, has had a wound on his leg for a long time, which keeps getting better and then worse again, because I can't keep him from running about till it is quite healed. As soon as it looks like healing, off he slips into the race with the other boys, or joins their excursions in hunting young antelopes. I have poulticed this boy's leg every day for at least two months. Sometimes I feel discouraged when I see it breaking out afresh, all through his own folly; though I know it is only like boys at home, and boys here are not under so much restraint as in England, and do not take so much notice of what is said to them.

"Add to these three cases a few more which my husband and I attended to the other morning. An old man with a sore throat, on which I put a wet cloth, and on the top of that a dry one, and gave him a dose of medicine, with certain other directions. A boy with a cold on the chest. A little boy to have two loose teeth pulled out. A Galla man with bad toes; and other cases. Sometimes there are more cases, sometimes less, and we have to do our best for all.

"Sometimes I think a professional man would be puzzled to know what to do in some instances. One day a man and his wife brought their little three-year-old child to be cured. They said he could not yet walk, and did not take notice of anything unless it was close to his eyes, although he appeared to be staring all the time. Poor little fellow! we at once saw that his case was beyond our power to assist, for he was a little idiot boy. His arms and ankles had numbers of heathenish charms, made of bits of wood, tied round them, and one piece was tied to a lock of hair on the crown of his head; but they had all proved to be of no use, although the Wanika put great faith in them. These people had come a two days' journey, and were obliged to return home again in sorrow, believing, as the man said, that the affliction was sent by God. The worst cases come from a distance; and, as they are generally of so many years standing, it is very difficult to know what to do with them. The people seem to think that a couple of doses of medicine ought to set them all right again. Some come to us nearly blind; others have had bad eyes for years; others come with the sight of one eye quite gone. Some come for medicine for their friends. A man has fallen out of a cocoa-nut tree; another has had a stab with a knife; some have smallpox, boils, rheumatism, and twenty other things which may amuse you to read about, but which I can hardly make up my mind to write about in a letter.

"I will, however, mention two cases of possession of evil spirits. The first is that of a young married woman. About a week ago a man came into the verandah; and showing a silver dollar, said he was hunting about for a white goat, and wanted to know if we had one that we would sell him? It must, however, be entirely white, with not a speck of black on it. Feeling my curiosity aroused, I asked him why he was so particular about its colour? and he told me the following story:—His sister, he said, had got an evil spirit. She could not eat; she could not sleep, nor walk, nor talk; but kept on all the time making a moaning noise. The evil spirit within her had asked for a white goat. They had offered it instead rice, and meal, and the best of food; but all were refused. It must have a white goat, and then it would depart. The goat was not to be killed; but was to be kept as an attendant on the woman wherever she went. If into the plantation, or to fetch water, or to gather firewood, it should still accompany her, and be to her as a guardian angel to protect her from all future evil. On being made acquainted that her brother was going out to seek this wonderful animal, the evil spirit in the woman was somewhat pacified, and allowed her to get a little sleep. The man appeared very desirous to succeed in obtaining his object. After having heard his story, our first remark was that his errand was all nonsense. Having asked some questions in reference to the patient, my husband at once offered to give him medicine for her, and was assured by the man that she should take it. 'Do you think,' said he 'that I want to throw my dollar away? Should I not suffer loss by the purchase of the goat? I prefer to take the medicine, if that will do as well.' So Mr. Wakefield gave him medicine, and the man went away, and soon came back again for 'more of the same kind.' My husband suggested waiting a day or two; and, as the man has not turned up again, I judge the devil has been driven out without having his desire for a white goat gratified. These desires are made known by the possessed one when the spirit is asked by the friends what it wants? So, of course, it is the inclination of the woman herself; for she well knows that at a time like this she can get whatever she likes to ask for.

"The other case is that of a man, and was rather a case of bewitchment. In this case, the man's younger brother came from Rabai to say that the invalid was suffering in his stomach, owing to his having been bewitched; and he desired assistance. It appears that this man had cheated another man of his wife, and being unwell some time afterwards, imagined that the man whom he had wronged had bewitched him. This, however, the man denied having done; but said, 'I will do it, though, through a Sawahili man from Pemba.' This threat was supposed to have been fulfilled by the man continuing ill. He then sent for the 'medicine man,' or sorcerer; and consulted with him about the matter. After various deliberations, this quack doctor proceeded to bleed the man at the stomach, and professed to take from him (1) some salt water, (2) a shell, and (3) a fish's tooth; thus proving, beyond all doubt, that the man was bewitched, and unquestionably by a man from the sea coast. The extraction of the above three things did not, however, give the man any relief, which accounted for his brother coming over here for

AN AFRICAN VILLAGE.

medicine. We gave him some, and we have heard no more of him.

"My husband has had a little trip of about thirty miles, there and back, to a village of the Wanika; and he staid one night away from home. The place visited was Duroomah, the native place of Mgomba, about six miles beyond Rabai. The people of Duroomah had, through Mgomba, expressed a strong wish to be visited by Mr. Wakefield, to make a palaver about 'the book,' what were the news it contained, and whether they might not be taught them as well as the people of Ribé. He could not say much during one visit, but talks of going again, and taking Nellie and me. He ate of the natives' food; slept in a hut without windows, and with only a low door to creep in at; and what made it more stifling was that it was the sleeping place of twenty or thirty goats, which were tied up all round the hut. The people were all very kind to him, and the visit did him good. While he was away, I had to start the hymns at morning and evening prayers; but the natives conducted the devotional exercises. Chai brought home a wild duck for dinner. It was the first I had seen here. It proved very tough eating, but as we had no meat in the house that day, we were very glad of it, though it was very small, and only like a chicken.

"Mr. Wakefield, Nellie, and I, recently had a ride of four miles to visit a district called Kinoonoona, where Kireri lives. We went at Kireri's request on a rather queer errand. Kireri married a heathen wife, paying twelve and a half dollars to her father as a sort of dowry. After he had had her two or three days she ran away home again, and refused to return to him. So our visit was with the object of trying to get the twelve and a half dollars back again, according to the custom of the country. Kireri thought I suppose, that the presence of a white man would show authority and power.

"At this place, I saw for the first time, a native doll, and tried very much to buy it; but the owner, a girl about thirteen years old, firmly refused to part with it. She said she wanted it for herself, and appeared to nurse it as if it were a real baby. It was made of a piece of wood, with a bit of cloth over the top, and with many beads sewn on for hair. Its dress consisted almost entirely of beads, but the doll itself had neither arms nor legs. I never knew before that the Wanika ever attempted to make dolls."

"Ribé, January 30th, 1873.—Two years ago, this month, I came up to Ribé, and it is nearly three years since I saw my dear friends in England. Oh, what a long time that seems. I dreamed the other night, when Mr. Wakefield was at Mombas, and Nellie and I were sleeping in the house alone, that she and I were in England, all among old friends. Nellie appeared to attract a good deal of attention from everybody; but, poor me, I looked and felt all *worn out*. I thought I looked in the glass and was amazed at my hollow cheeks and protruding cheek bones, while everybody was speaking of me as being, at least, forty years of age! I think the shock awoke me, for when I opened my eyes there were no signs of daybreak, and the little lamp at my side only 'made darkness more visible,' while outside I could not tell how near roamed the 'pilgrims of the night.'

"We have had a visitor from England since I wrote last. On Saturday, December 14th, while I was teaching some of the boys to write, at a table in the verandah, a man came up the path with a letter for my husband. It took us very much by surprise, as it was written from Mombas and signed J. W. Hicks. In it the writer said 'I am a natural history collector, and, having come out from England, Dr. Kirk has recommended me to come up to Ribé at once, as being cooler than Zanzibar at the present time.' And then, to our astonishment, the man seemed in a great hurry for an answer, saying that the Musungu was down at the landing place waiting for him. I at once told the boys to clear away their writing materials; and set them to work to clean the iron house, put in tables, chairs, etc., while I made other necessary arrangements for the comfort of our expected guest. I got a sheep killed for food for the next day, (Sunday,) and as long as it would keep good: while my husband got the donkey ready, and sent it down by Tofiki to meet Mr. Hicks. They met him on the way coming up, and soon he was here and greeting us. He was of dark complexion, hair, and eyes; age twenty-three—and a native of Gosport, near Portsmouth. He spoke of a widowed mother of whom he was the chief support, and a sister about twenty; and when I played and sang, he said his sister sang some of the same pieces.

"Of course we had many questions to ask him about England; but he knew none of our friends.

"Mr. H. was our guest for a week, after which, as he intended staying for some months, it was thought best that his own servant, an English-speaking native of Zanzibar, should cater for him, and we shared the cooking kitchen together. His usual plan was to get an early breakfast, and then start out into the sunshine, with his butterfly-net in his hand, and his servant behind him, carrying a tin box, (in which to receive his spoils,) and a double-barrelled gun, loaded with very small shot, for shooting birds. Then 'bang,' bang,' would go the gun, and in two or three hours he would return, go into the iron house, and commence skinning and stuffing his birds. Then he would lie down and get a nap, by and by his dinner, and then occasionally take another short sally; but more usually this finished the day's work. He would then sit in the verandah till sun-down, (six p.m.,) and at the lighting of the lamps or candles, always came in with us to tea, and remained with us until bedtime, joining with us in our evening family worship.

"When Mr. Hicks had been here about a month at his occupation, buying little snakes, frogs, lizards, etc., etc., for pence, of the natives; putting them into spirits, in addition to offering the boys money to bring him beetles, or, in fact, any living thing; he was suddenly seized with an attack of the spleen, and he awoke us in the night with his groans. My husband at once got up and went to him, and gave him medicine. He had to keep his bed for two or three days, but seemed to get gradually better. Then he was seized with a difficulty of breathing—asthma, or something of that kind, and panted to get his breath. We exerted ourselves in every possible way in attendance on him at all times, but his disease seemed to have fast hold upon him, and three days ago he left us for Zanzibar and England.

"On Christmas day it was decided to have the usual feast for the people; and, as Mr. Wakefield was very poorly, our English visitor helped me well in making the arrangements. The decorating of the school-room with such beautiful evergreens as you cannot buy for money in Old England was finished the day before, and very early on Christmas morning the boys and some of the men were busy cutting down and bringing branches for decorating the verandah. The beautiful fronds of the palm tree displayed their elegant form when nailed against the white walls of the house, while the pillars that support the roof were all twined about like Maypoles, so that when finished the verandah looked as snug and verdant as a fairy bower. While the boys were decorating the verandah our visitor and I went to the fold, and chose out two large sheep and a good fat goat; and, while they were being killed, I dealt out the rice from my store to the native women on the Station, who each took their share in cooking and preparing the food for the feast. The rice was flavoured with the milk squeezed from the grated inside of the cocoanut, about thirty cocoa-nuts being required for the purpose.

"Long tables were set up in the verandah, and forms and planks placed on each side for seats, the tables being covered with a piece of new calico by way of table-cloth. When the tables had been fixed, some of the little black children brought me some beautiful wild flowers they had gathered, as their contribution towards the decorations. This reminded me so much of a custom we had on 'breaking-up day' at school in England that I determined to make a wreath of the flowers for Nellie. I did so, and this pleased her much, and was much admired by the other children, who had probably never seen a garland of flowers before in their lives. Soon such a party of little black boys and girls came round me, and one little girl said, in her native tongue, 'Please, lady, make *me* one; I can find plenty more flowers.' Then another shyly said, 'And *I* should like one too;' and the rest all looked up and begged with their eyes. So I sent them all away to gather what they could, and soon I was busy with such a collection of flowers as would have been highly prized in England on Christmas Day. Most of them were scarlet, and very much like the scarlet verbena. These, with a few smaller varieties of different colours, mixed with a beautiful snowy-white star-flower, which grows in abundance in the hedgerow bounding the path to the Mission, and smells very sweetly, showed well together on the black foreheads of the little boys and girls, and their little heads did as well as vases of flowers at the tables.

"We ourselves dined earlier than the people, and in our own English way. 'Did you get any mince-pies?' No; but we can have 'happy months' this year without mince-pies! *The secret of being happy here is in trying to make others happy.*

"About five o'clock in the afternoon the feast was ready. All the largest dishes, plates, and trays that could be found were used to pile the boiled rice upon, and when placed upon the tables they looked like a long row of huge white ant-hills. Between each little rice mountain was a large basin full of meat and gravy, to eat with the rice. After all the people had assembled and taken their seats at the long tables, they stood up and sang 'Praise God from whom all blessings flow,' by way of giving thanks, and after that I assure you they did not need any inviting to commence. Spoons and plates are not considered necessary here. Three or four of those nearest to each dish join at it, and have all things common. With a piece of meat in one hand and a ball of rice in the other, which they dip into the gravy basin, they go working away, one hand up and the other hand down, popping it in and losing no time, until they can positively eat no more. Then we gave them as much sweet sherbet, made of honey and sugar and water, as they could drink. At length all were *fully* satisfied, and we adjourned to the school-room and sang some Christmas hymns, and heard a short address from Mr. Wakefield about the Babe of Bethlehem. The sun had now set, so the school-room was lighted by a beautiful lamp given to my husband before he left England. The room was nearly full, and the crowd of black faces all looking so smiling and shining and happy made me feel quite happy too. May we and they all one day join in the angels' song round the throne of God and the Lamb for ever and ever!

"When the people had all said 'Good night,' Mr. Wakefield and I and our English friend came into the house and spent the evening in a quiet manner, talking, over a cup of tea, of bygone Christmases, and of dear old England and our friends there. Then, at our visitor's request, I sang and played 'Do they miss me at home?' 'Home, sweet home,' 'Dear home,' and one or two Christmas pieces, and then we all retired."

"February 1st.—Mr. Wakefield and I are often very much amused at Nellie and her ways. She is getting so plump and strong, and likes to sit on my knee and play the piano, and sing. At prayers and at service on Sunday her little voice frequently rises above all the rest, causing many a smile as she stands on a chair by my side, holding the manuscript hymn book in both hands, and looking at it so earnestly. Then, too, her loud 'Amen' at the prayer is clearly distinguishable; sometimes she gives the response when everybody else is silent, all the time kneeling, with her little hands covering her eyes, and then I really can't help feeling tickled, she says the word so very plainly. At night, too, before she goes to bed she says, in very broken style, after me,—

'Gentle Jesus, meek and mild,'

and afterwards she always prays for 'Unk Obber.' Guess who that is, if you can. I have seen her kneel down to pray alone at different times during the day. One day she went with me into the bath room, and while I was washing, she kneeled down against the chair and put her head down, but all I heard was the ' Amen ' at the end."

" February 15th.—Mr. Wakefield is sending home the first Local Preachers' Plan of the Ribé Circuit. Six or seven young men go out every Sunday to the little villages and hamlets round about here to give the people the message of salvation, and invite them all to chapel. They often get very much laughed at, and the people are very fond of trying to joke with them about hell fire, etc. One Sunday I was very much amused at a remark made by a couple of old folks who were sitting by their hut, to whom the invitation had been given to come and hear the Word. ' Yes,' said the old man, ' I am willing to come when I hear the news that you people who read the book *don't die*, but at present I see no advantage between you and ourselves.' The young evangelist then told him that there were two kinds of death, and that although our bodies die, as is proved by poor Butterworth's grave close to our house, yet he had *eternal* life to offer them. But these poor Wanika care only for the present."

" Ribé, March 24th, 1873.—Sir Bartle Frere and a large party of gentlemen came up to Ribé to see us, on Saturday last, and left us this morning. On Thursday evening a soldier came to our door carrying a letter from Sir Bartle's secretary, which stated that his excellency and suite had just arrived at Mombas, and intended coming on to see us at Ribé the next morning. I cannot express how surprised and delighted we were that, in our lonely wilderness home, we were so soon to be gladdened with the sight of pleasant faces from dear old England, and especially that we were to be honoured with such distinguished visitors ; and we set to work at once to make the best preparations we could for their reception.

"The next day we had just finished our preparations, and had hoisted our little English flag on the station, when our visitors made their appearance. Sir Bartle was the first to arrive, and we soon found that he was a most charming, kind, and genial gentleman. He spoke to me very kindly, and said, 'We shall soon be old friends.' The Secretary of Legation came next, then Captain Fairfax, commander of the *Enchantress*, and then by degrees stepped forward more tall, officer-like gentlemen—majors, lieutenants, colonels, captains, etc., whose names I need not mention. Altogether the party consisted of thirteen English gentlemen and five servants, besides more than fifty soldiers sent by the Governor of Mombas as an escort. This was a large increase to the population of Ribé all at once, and made no small stir and excitement at the mission station. The English gentlemen had brought all their own provisions with them, which were cooked and prepared by their own servants; while I looked after the fifty soldiers by selecting goats and sheep to be slaughtered, and by dealing out rice without measure to be cooked for them, so that I was kept pretty busy for the time.

"On Saturday a large number of the most important of the natives of Ribé and the neighbourhood assembled in front of the mission-house, and went through a number of war-dances and other strange performances, flourishing their swords in the air, and making the most horrible noises and shrieks, to the no small astonishment and amusement of our English visitors. After this a target was set up, and prizes were offered to the Wanika for the best shots with bows and arrows. Then the English officers practised with their rifles, and this astonished the natives wonderfully, who were compelled to acknowledge themselves thoroughly beaten when they saw the unerring aim of the English at such immense distances.

"On Sunday Sir Bartle attended the Sunday-school and preaching service in our humble school-room; and himself gave a nice address to the people, which my husband trans-

lated to them, and which pleased them very much. After
the address to the people, one of our young men said to our
distinguished guest, 'We thank you very much, sir, for your
words; they are very good, and they have filled our hearts
with joy.' And another added, 'And may God bless you
very much.' Some of the people remarked afterwards that
these Wasungoo were quite a different race of white men
from what they had ever seen before, they were so tall. They
said, 'They looked as strong as lions.'

"We learned with much regret from Mrs. Kirk that our
English friend, Mr. Hicks, fell a victim to the terrible climate of East Africa in January, only a week after his arrival
at Zanzibar. Mrs. Kirk says, 'He lived during the few days
he remained here at the French Mission, and they were very
kind to him, and did all that could be done for him. Dr.
Huran, from the Flag-ship, also attended him, but nothing
could have saved him at that stage of his disease. One lung
was quite gone and directly the disease spread to the other
he died. I had a few pencil lines from him in the evening;
and one of my boys who took him some jelly saw him. He
went off quietly in his sleep that night, 'poor fellow.'"

"April 18th, 1873.—My piano is a very great curiosity in
this wild part of Africa. At first the people came in such numbers to see it and hear it played that they became quite
troublesome. They would rush in and fill the house, and
then we found it difficult to get them out again; there were
so many other things they wanted to look at, and have explained. They must needs touch everything with their dirty,
greasy hands; sit down in all the chairs to see if they were
comfortable, and ask endless questions about everything
around them. I think after the piano the thing which makes
them laugh the loudest is the sight of Nellie's doll, which
they fancy must be alive. Some of the folks are so alarmed
that they rush out of the house in a fright. One woman
held her hands quite tightly over her eyes until she thought
we had put it away, and shrunk back as though it might

have been a serpent. Up-grown men have come many miles to see it. The cuckoo clock is also a great novelty, and also a small musical box we have.

"The Wanika are now looking out for the rainy season, and they say it is long in coming, 'because the white man is *building*.' They have been performing superstitious nonsense to persuade the rain to come, such as removing the bones of certain dead men to a place of greater sanctity, killing sheep in sacrifice, and so on. They know that if the rain does not come soon to make the corn grow there will be a famine. But they do not pray to the Almighty, and are to be pitied.

"We get thoroughly worn out at this time of the year. I could not help saying to Mr. Wakefield yesterday after I had done my hair at the glass and had observed my hollow, pale cheeks, 'I don't believe the people at home would know me if they were to see me now.'

"The thermometer has been standing at 90° or 91° in the shade; and this heat, with not a leaf stirring, is to us cold-country folk, rather melting. I have to keep a fan by my bed-side, and every now and then snatch it up and give myself a few good whiffs by way of relief.

"Just now is the season, too, when the lions come near us. Only the day before yesterday I heard that they had visited a place a few miles from us and carried off a man, besides injuring a great many others."

We now come to the last letter written by Mrs. Wakefield's own hand, some extracts from which will close this chapter.

"May 30th, 1873.—When I last wrote we were suffering the intense heat of our 'hot season:' now the weather has entirely changed, and we are having the unhealthy wet season with all the mists, vapours, and malaria rising out of the valleys and jungle which surround us. I am glad to make daily use of that thick, grey, woollen shawl of mother's,—the most useful article we brought out here. Nellie, too, wears a blue French-merino paletot, lined with wadding, and which covers her from neck to ankles, and I am busy making her some flannel vests to keep out the cold and damp from her little chest. The natives themselves get very bad coughs and colds at this season of the year. Even we sometimes envy them their bright fires in their little huts of an evening, for they look so snug and comfortable, while our little cottage is feeling all damp and cold and consequently unhealthy.

"Nellie is getting very precocious, and it is almost impossible to say anything in her presence without her little ladyship making some remark or asking some question on the subject. I am sorry to say, however, that she talks very little in English, although she understands it perfectly well. I was somewhat amused the day before yesterday while watching her and her little nigger friends in the verandah. They were playing at tending cows. Nellie, esteeming herself the eldest of the party, was of course the cowherd, and with a long stick in hand was driving before her five little nude niggers, who were crawling along before her on their hands and knees, she all the time calling my attention to what she was doing, with evident satisfaction, and expecting a word of admiration at the state of her herd, which of course I bestowed.

"I now enclose a letter which I forgot to put in my last. It contains a few 'lines' from Nellie to Uncle Robert, which were written for his birthday, without a word of suggestion on my part. At her own request I gave her the pencil and paper, and also send it to you by her orders. To make sure that the wrong person should not get it she pointed to your likeness while giving me the needful directions.

"The man who is to carry this letter to Mombas sits before me out of patience at waiting so long. Love to Uncle William and all friends. Now once more adieu. *God bless you*, my own dear brother.

I remain, as ever,
Your very loving Sister,
REBECCA."

CHAPTER XIV.

Illness and Death.

ON Sunday morning, June 8th, 1873, a bright, beautiful day, the loving family at Ribé was gladdened by the addition to its number of a fine, handsome, little boy, whom his parents named Bertie, and whom Nellie, delighted beyond measure to welcome, insisted on claiming as her own special and peculiar property, and introducing as such to the native visitors on all fitting occasions.

This new-born joy, however, was but the harbinger of swift and deeply wounding sorrows, that, in a few sad weeks were to rob this bright, sunny home of all its gladness, and leave it, like the fire-swept hills and valleys among which it now and again stood, a charred and blackened desolation; one tiny flower and drooping tree alone remaining to survive the painful ordeal.

To relate the story of Mrs. Wakefield's last illness and death is almost all that remains to be done; and for the mournful particulars which will now be laid before the reader, I am indebted solely to the minute and carefully written journal of this sorrowful time, kept from day to day, amid the greatest possible difficulties, by her devoted husband.

Of the nature of Mrs. Wakefield's illness, and of the progress of the diseases which terminated in her removal from earth, little need be said here. Exhausting fever, accompanied by long continued delirium, painful and virulent abscesses, paralyzing rheumatism, pain and swelling of the face, and excessive weakness, following closely upon the event to which reference has been made, were amongst the foes with which a naturally strong and vigorous constitution, joined with a hopeful and even vivacious disposition, bravely battled for about six weeks, and before which, just as gleams of returning strength began to dawn, she ultimately succumbed.

During the whole of this time, her noble and devoted husband was her only medical attendant, no other medical or surgical assistance being within reach; and during the greater part of the time he was, day and night, her only nurse. The native women have no idea whatever of rendering such gentle, tender attentions as an invalid requires; and, excepting the infirm Mr. Rebmann at Mombas, there were no Europeans in the country within a distance of a hundred and forty miles.

It was on Friday, June 13th, that the first alarming symptoms in Mrs. Wakefield's illness appeared; and, on the day following, Saturday, her husband was gladdened by the unexpected arrival of a Christian native woman from the Church Mission Station at Rabai, who had been educated at a Christian Training Institution at Bombay. Her name was Polly; and, as soon as she had heard the news of Mrs. Wakefield's illness, she had left her husband and come over to Ribé to offer her assistance as nurse. This was exceedingly kind: but their united efforts to stay the disease were unavailing.

A week later, still darker clouds seemed to gather; and almost all hope of her restoration seemed to be cut off. "On Thursday evening, June 19th," says Mr. Wakefield, "as she was lying in bed, and I had just finished the duties of the day, Mrs. Wakefield said to me rather sadly, *There is one thing which I ought to tell you. It is this. Though I have prayed a great deal for recovery, yet all seems dark.*'" He continues—"These words sank like lead into my heart, for they were in exact accordance with my own experience. I told her so. 'But then,' I added, 'God may be simply trying our faith: you know it is His way sometimes.' Very feebly and with evident doubt, she replied, ' Y—e—s ; it may be so, but I don't know.' I think I soothed her; but it was a dark hour for us both, and that, too, so early in her illness." He adds, "During the whole of Mrs. Wakefield's illness my prayers for her recovery were frequent and earnest; and, when I had impressions of her possible removal, they were prayers of agony and tears. I retired to the iron house, where no one could possibly see me, and poured out my soul to God as I never prayed before. I pleaded the Divine promise. 'The prayer of faith shall save the sick, and the Lord shall raise him up,' and I held on firmly to that promise. Sometimes through the darkness there were faint gleams of an answer; but I was never fully satisfied, although I continued to hope on until the day of her death."

On Sunday, June 22nd, she was too weak to move herself as she lay in bed. Her husband asked her if she were weaker than yesterday, and she said, " Yes." Her voice was very weak and low, but she tried to sing part of a Kinika translation of the hymn

"Jesus Christ is risen to-day ; Alleluia,"

of which the following are the first verses of the original:—

> Ha uwal Kesa be Jasus, Alleluya
> Ha dua ha diète, Alleluya
> Yo in Muke iridue, Alleluya
> Yo 'n fara Kesa nu pasa, Alleluya.
>
> Midagamu dakach suni, Alleluya
> Midagamu gangesa, Alleluya
> Midagamu egusani, Alleluya
> Ha chabse chufana uwala, Alleluya.

and when, through weakness, her voice failed, Mr. Wakefield sung it for her. She wept when she felt how weak and helpless she was.

The next morning the fever was somewhat abated, and

she appeared better. She smiled on Nellie, and took Bertie from the nurse; but soon afterwards there was a relapse, and the delirium returned.

During the whole of this week there was much fever and delirium; but in the lucid intervals her weakness and pain were so great as to prevent her entering into any connected conversation.

On Sunday, June 29th, Mrs. Wakefield was entirely free from mental aberrations, and, being apparently a little better, sat up for a short time, while her husband was able to conduct the Sabbath school and the usual preaching service. The night following passed quietly away, and even in her sleep her low sweet voice was often heard engaged in prayer, in a calm and rational manner.

On Tuesday, July 1st, Polly, the nurse, was compelled to return home. It was harvest time, and she had been but ill spared during the time she had already spent at Ribé, and now her husband had come to take her home. Mrs. Wakefield sat up for a little in the afternoon, and when she wished Polly 'good-bye' she gave her a little present, and thanked her very much for her kindness to herself and the children. Polly promised to return to Ribé as soon as possible.

Mr. Wakefield was now the sole nurse and attendant of his wife and the children, the younger of whom, Bertie, was now also in a critical condition, and his incessant labours and anxiety on their behalf may be better imagined than described. His sad, careworn appearance, as well as Nellie's frail condition at this time, led his weak and helpless companion to observe, "*Perhaps the Lord is about to take us all to heaven together.*" Day and night he was ever at her side, seldom completing his daily duties on her behalf till between two and three o'clock in the morning, when he sat down to make a few notes of the previous day's proceedings, and then threw himself down for a brief rest, before commencing the watching and nursing of another day.

"On Wednesday, July the 2nd," writes Mr. Wakefield,

"I got Mrs. W. into the sitting room about ten a.m., where she sat at breakfast with Nellie and me. It was almost a formal attendance, as she ate very little indeed. She drank a little coffee. She sat as long as she could, and then I carried her to the sofa and laid her down, when she fell asleep. When she awoke she asked me to read something to her. I took up one of our Connexional Magazines, which had arrived from England a few days before, and read to her. She soon afterwards fell asleep again, and slept soundly for the whole of the afternoon."

On Friday, July 4th, she dictated her last letter to her brother. It was, as ever, full of sisterly affection, and was written in a buoyant, hopeful spirit; for she had not yet given up that anticipation of her ultimate recovery, to which she tenaciously clung almost to the end. She hoped, she said, to write him a long letter herself as soon as her strength should permit. This was her last message to any of her friends, for the reason above intimated.

Sunday, July 6th, was the last Sabbath but one of her life. Mr. Wakefield says, "This was another day of extreme weakness. Mrs. W. urged me to leave her, and go to open the school: and again in the afternoon, she desired me to go and hold the usual preaching service. I did both. In the evening she spoke despairingly about ever gaining strength any more. I spoke to her of the Divine ability, willingness, and promise, and endeavoured to encourage her. She asked me to give her the Life of John Hunt, the Wesleyan Missionary, to read, and she lingered over its pages with deep interest. This was the last book but one she read. She sometimes, after this, asked me to give her her Bible, evidently preferring it to all other books. That Bible is well marked."

On Thursday, July the 10th, she was exceedingly prostrate; but lay on the sofa in the sitting-room most of the day. In the evening, when about to remove her to the bedroom, her husband gently raised her from the sofa, and she stood for a few moments, strongly supported by his arms.

She then began to pray, and prayed very earnestly for strength and patience, and for submission to the Divine will. She said " O Lord, I should like to live for my dear husband's sake, and for the children's sake, and for the sake of Thy work: but, if Thou hast other purposes, not my will, but Thine, O Lord, be done. Amen." Her husband then assisted her to the bed-room, with feelings it would be impossible to describe.

"The next day, Friday, she remained in bed for the whole day. When, during the morning, her husband urged her to take a dose of medicine, which he hoped would do her good, and which he was holding out to her in a spoon, she at first refused to take it, saying "We do not know whether it is God's will to raise me up again." Her husband urged that, whatever the case might be, it was their duty to do all they could to promote her recovery. She replied "Certainly," and took the dose. Her mind wandered considerably during this and the next two days.

On Saturday morning, July 12th, little Bertie died. This was a sore trial. With a breaking heart, Mr. Wakefield had now to perform the very delicate task of informing his suffering wife of their great sorrow, and of comforting her under this great affliction. He says "I told her that the Lord had taken our little one to Himself; that it was really His, not ours; that He had taken it to heaven to dwell among the angels, and that it was supremely and eternally blessed. That it would never sin, and that it would never be exposed to any danger; but that in every respect it was safe for ever. She asked that the babe might be given to her, and pressed it to her bosom with true maternal affection; but finding that it was indeed lifeless, she handed it back to me again."

What remains of this sorrowful day's history will be best told in Mr. Wakefield's own words.

"In the evening, when the coffin was ready, I brought it into the bed-room, and laid little Bertie in it. I got Mrs. Wakefield up with great difficulty, and dressed her, and she sat upon the edge of the bed. Her tender, motherly love wanted to do something in assisting me with the preparations, and she made several efforts; but her right arm, for some time paralyzed by rheumatism, was now utterly powerless. After laying Bertie in his last narrow bed, my wife took a last look at her babe, and I carried him into the next room. When I returned to her she put something into my hand, and told me to lay it in the coffin, on Bertie's breast. It was *a few African wild flowers*, and the sight touched my heart. When I had fulfilled her request, I came back to her side, and sitting down by her on the bed put my arm round her to support her. What her feelings were at that time I cannot tell: she did not weep; on the contrary, one more calm and subdued I never saw. Then she breathed forth one of the sweetest and most touching prayers I ever heard. It was quiet, devout, complete! and her spirit seemed completely bathed in calm and devout feeling. The following sentences of the prayer are all I can remember. 'O LORD, LOOK MERCIFULLY UPON US IN OUR GREAT AFFLICTION. THOU HAST SORELY TRIED US. ONE SORROW HAS COME UPON ANOTHER. BUT, O LORD, IF THOU CANST, STAY NOW THY HAND, AND LET US LEARN ALL THAT THOU WOULDEST TEACH US BY THIS DISPENSATION. HEAL AND COMFORT US. SPARE AND RAISE ME UP AGAIN, IF IT BE IN ACCORDANCE WITH THY PURPOSE; BUT, IF NOT, NOT MY WILL, BUT THINE, O LORD, BE DONE. AMEN.' The whole of this prayer was uttered very distinctly but faintly, the 'Amen' quietly melting away at the end.

"The daylight was now fading, and, having gently laid my wife down, I left her, to perform the funeral ceremonies of my child. While one of the boys tolled the bell, I took Nellie by the hand, and led her into the chapel. This was hard work. With great difficulty I read the service in the chapel, and then we slowly proceeded to the grave; Nellie and I following the coffin as chief mourners, the boys and the mission people completing the procession. Here I buried our darling boy beside the grave of Mr. Butterworth. Nellie and I and the rest cast our flowers into the grave, and we came away; the people to get their suppers and go to bed, and I to light up our gloomy cottage, and to sit beside my dying wife. We wept together as we conversed about our great loss, and I afterwards read to her the xc. Psalm, and prayed with her. Then about one a.m., thoroughly exhausted, I lay down to rest."

Sunday, July 13th, was my sister's last Sabbath on earth. In the morning she looked at her husband in great sorrow, and, bursting into tears, said " I have no baby now." He tried to comfort her as best he could. During the day, an attempt was made to remove her to the sitting-room for change of air, but she was too weak to leave her bed any more. She was very pale, and thin, and weak.

At eleven o'clock in the evening, Mr. Wakefield sat down beside her and read to her the cii. Psalm. She seemed much to enjoy the reading, and commented intelligently on every verse. At the 7th verse "I watch, and am alone as a sparrow upon the house-top," her husband paused, and said to her, " That is I," when she replied " Ay, that it is." At the 15th verse, " So shall the heathen fear the name of the Lord," Mr. Wakefield said " What a blessed time it will be when all Africa shall fear the name of the Lord; but the time *will come* when even the heathen Wanika round about us will become his people." She said " Yes," and was evidently much pleased by the thought. There was a sweet tranquil smile on her countenance during the whole of the reading. Mr. Wakefield then prayed; and she seemed to join in every petition, and to accompany her husband right to the throne of grace.

Mr. Wakefield's health had suffered greatly; and he now began to fear that he should not be able to survive the shock that he too well dreaded would soon fall upon him. On Monday morning, however, to his great joy, Polly, the nurse, returned from Rabai, and rendered him very valuable assistance in his overwhelming duties, until **that assistance was no longer required.**

On that morning, Monday, July 14th, very early, Mrs. Wakefield had gone back in thought to her early home at Mountsorrel, and fancied that once more she was surrounded by her old friends there. After a time the illusion was dispelled, and her husband bathed her head with cool wet cloths. This was delicious to the poor fever-stricken patient. Mr. Wakefield asked her if it were not so, and she replied, " Oh, yes ; very much so; thank you, many, many times, my dear." At another time, she playfully observed that it were almost worth her while to be ill to receive so many kind attentions. She was, throughout her whole illness, excessively grateful for all that was done for her, and never uttered one word of murmuring or complaint from the commencement of her affliction to its close. She was in a joyous frame of mind during the whole of this day, although the feverish state of the brain caused a good deal of mental wandering.

Some of the most alarming symptoms had now been checked, and the virulence of the disease brought under; so that, with the assistance which had now returned to hand, Mr. Wakefield began to hope that if the patient's strength could only hold out for a few days longer, there would be a fair prospect of her ultimate recovery; to promote which, he and the nurse were now able to give their undivided attention.

On Tuesday, July 15th, there was a good deal of delirious wandering during most of the day ; which, in the evening, somewhat abated. About ten o'clock in the evening, while Mr. Wakefield was in the sitting-room, making a few hasty notes of the day's proceedings, he heard her sweet soft voice begin to sing, in the Galla language, the following verses of a hymn which the people commonly sing in the chapel at the time of evening prayer :

> "Gar kena irana, irana kilkila,
> Hin tenu laf tana, safara tolchina
> Ulele in k'amna,—jaben ka irana,—
> Nuf Wain wol injira, nu gad iyana.

> Gar kena irana, bad'e tan hin tenu,
> Laf tun d'ukuba, aram hindandenu;
> Harian tena d'ud'u inum d'ut'i,—
> Ammo iran kena fayam ta duri."

The following is a literal translation of the Galla verses,—

> "Our home is in heaven, high up in the sky,
> We do not dwell here, we journey away;
> We have (our) staves (strength from above),
> God is with us, let us all depart.

> "Our home is in heaven, we do not love this world,
> A world of sickness, we cannot stay here:
> Our friends, all of them are dying,
> But in our home above there is undecaying health."

Mr. Wakefield says, "I had often heard my dear wife sing sweetly; but never before with such exquisite feeling, tenderness, and pathos. She was evidently very happy. She sang as though she were already with the angels, or as if she were having an enrapturing glimpse of the glories of heaven. After the hymn was sung she began to pray, and I stole softly to her bedside. Her eyes were closed, and she was entirely unconscious of my presence, as I stood there bending over her. The chief burden of her prayer was for a higher Christian character; for greater devotedness to God; for greater usefulness, and in the end, for everlasting life. The following were among its petitions, 'O LORD MAKE US MORE HOLY; MORE LIKE CHRIST. MAY WE BE FAR IN ADVANCE OF OTHERS IN HOLINESS; NOT FOR THE SAKE OF OUTSTRIPPING THEM, BUT FOR THE SAKE OF THE HOLINESS ITSELF.'

"A serene smile as of celestial sweetness and gentleness suffused her countenance, which was beautifully in harmony with her prayer; and the whole prayer was breathed with such a burning fervour that her soul seemed to be the subject of a direct inspiration from heaven."

"When she had finished," Mr. Wakefield continues, "she quietly breathed '*Amen.*' I then bent over and kissed her, and earnestly responded ' Amen ' too. She then desired me to pray, which I did; beseeching the Divine pity on her in her sufferings and weakness; praying for her speedy restoration to health and to her work, and that her own prayer for increased holiness and devotedness to God might be heard and answered. She followed me sentence by sentence to the end, and then clearly said ' Amen.' Soon after this I gave her a drink of water, and her mind wandered again."

We have now come to the last day of Mrs. Wakefield's stay on earth,—Wednesday, July the 16th. She rested well during the previous night, but in the morning looked extremely thin, weak, and exhausted. The delirium and sleeplessness of the preceding days and nights had robbed her of her little remaining strength; but she appeared to be quite free from pain. Once during the morning she called to her husband, and said that she was falling. He at once took hold of her and told her she should not fall, when she clasped his hands quite tightly, smiled gratefully, and said "Thank you." At another time, thankful for Mr. Wakefield's presence, and perhaps foreseeing the parting that was now at hand, she said fervently, " Oh Tom, my *dear* Tom."

Soon after this, partly owing to the dryness of her tongue and throat, and partly from excessive weakness, she entirely lost all power of audible speech. Her husband moistened her lips, and listened most intently to many efforts which she now made to communicate something to him; but to his great grief and disappointment the words were utterly inaudible. She made many efforts to speak, but failed in all.

In the afternoon, about three o'clock, as he stood by her bedside, Mr. Wakefield said to her, "Is there anything you would like, that I could get you, my dear?" There was no response. He then said "The Lord is with you, dear, and He can raise you up again if He likes; for He has all power." She made an effort to say "Yes." Mr. Wakefield continued, "He will never leave you. He will never forsake you," when she rounded her lips as much as possible to say "No."

About half-past four o'clock in the afternoon she turned her eyes fully and intelligently upon her husband, and indicated, as well as she could, that she wished to kiss him. He then bent over her, when she did as he had supposed, and looked pleased. He then brought Nellie to her side, and she looked earnestly and affectionately upon her. He continues "I then lifted her up for her mamma to kiss her, when she lovingly kissed the child. This was a bright little interval, but it was terribly like saying 'Good-bye.' It was her last loving adieu to earth, as she was consciously advancing toward the bright spirit-world. It was the gentle raising of the anchor, which for nearly twenty-nine years had held her to this world of sin and suffering and sorrow; the quiet unmooring of the bark which was now calmly but triumphantly gliding into the desired haven."

Putting Nellie down, and looking at his dying companion, Mr. Wakefield now sung softly to her some verses of a hymn that has often been upon the lips of the saints in their last hours.

> "Jesus, lover of my soul,
>   Let me to Thy bosom fly :
> While the nearer waters roll,
>   While the tempest still is high.
>
> "Hide me, O my Saviour hide,
>   Till the storm of life be past ;
> Safe into the haven guide ;
>   O receive my soul at last."

He then said to her, "Jesus is with you now: I know He is; He will never leave you; He will never forsake you." A peaceful smile was upon her countenance, and she at once formed her lips to say "Oh no." He continued, "He has been with you in your health and strength, and He will not leave you in your weakness and affliction. He will not leave you to struggle alone in the trying hour. He is with you now, is He not?" She made another effort to say "YES." He suggested,

> "Jesus can make a dying bed
> Feel soft as downy pillows are,
> While on His breast I lean my head,
> And breathe my soul out sweetly there,"

and continued "What a precious blessing it is to have Jesus with us in a dying hour. None can comfort and sustain like Him, and He will go with you all the way. We can only go with you to the brink of Jordan, and there, on the margin, we are compelled to leave you. But He will go with you through the dark river. He will hold up your head, that the waters shall not overflow you, and will bear you safely and triumphantly to the other side. Hundreds of years ago the Psalmist could joyfully exclaim 'Yea, though I walk through the valley of the shadow of death, I will fear no evil, for thou art with me; Thy rod and Thy staff they comfort me.' If the Psalmist could thus confidently speak and sing, in reference to the comfort and support of the Divine presence in the last hour, how much more may the devout Christian do so under the fuller and clearer light of the Gospel. You will soon be in heaven, and there you will see your father, and mother, and Iliffe, and John (Mitchil), and others."

As long as she was able Mrs. Wakefield seemed to express approval of the kind and comforting words that were being spoken to her. There was no fear in her countenance, but a strong consciousness that she was resting upon the Rock of Ages.

The natives residing on the Station, Gallas, Wanika, and Wasawahili were now admitted to take a last look at their dying friend. As they stood by her bedside, Mr. Wakefield reminded them of how much she had undergone for their sakes; of her leaving home and friends in England, and particularly her only and well-beloved brother; of the long, comfortless, tempestuous voyage across the ocean; of her trials at Zanzibar; of the rough passage to Mombas; of the discomforts of the house there; of her successive attacks of fever at Ribé, and of her great sufferings in other respects. "All this," he continued, "has been bravely, and without a murmur, endured for your sakes. For you who are standing around her dying bed, she has sacrificed comfort, health, friends, brother, home, and all that is bright and joyous, and borne the burden and heat of a fever-stricken country. She can no longer speak to you; but if she could do so, she would even now tell you to love Jesus, to give yourselves to Him, to live for heaven, and follow her to the home and rest to which she is going." After this address the people retired.

Soon after sunset that evening it became evident that the last conflict was at hand, and at ten minutes after seven o'clock, with her right hand firmly clasped by those of her husband's, Mrs. Wakefield calmly drew her last breath, and passed away from her work on earth to her reward in heaven.

The funeral took place on the afternoon of the day following, Thursday, July 17th. Mr. Wakefield was compelled to superintend all the preparations for the interment himself, but was assisted in the conduct of the service by George David, an educated native Catechist from Rabai, to whom reference has already been made. Mr. Wakefield thus tells the sorrowful story: "Just before the coffin lid was closed down I took a last look at my dearest earthly friend. I kissed the marble forehead and said 'Farewell,' and then called for Nellie. I lifted the little one up for a last look at her mamma, when she said, 'Kiss, kiss.' (Let me kiss her.) She bent down, and her little rosy lips kissed those of her now sainted mother.

"We both placed some African wild flowers upon her bosom, and the form of her who had been my companion in many difficulties and trials, my solace in many a sorrow, my help in many a weak hour, and my helpmate for several years in my blessed work, vanished from my sight.

"I painted on the lid of the coffin, with ink, the words,

REBECCA,

WIFE OF THE

REV. T. WAKEFIELD,

Died July 16th, 1875,

Aged 28 Years.

"At about a quarter past two in the afternoon we commenced the procession to the chapel, Nellie and I walking as chief mourners immediately behind the coffin, which was carried in calico slings, by six native Christians. The chapel was crowded with people. Many were there who had never before stepped inside our little sanctuary. I read the Burial Service from our Connexional 'Book of Services.' From beginning to end the service was baptized in tears.

"After George David had offered prayer, the mournful procession moved along the verandah to the grave. Nellie had a bandaged foot, and I was afraid I should have to carry her; but the little darling managed to toddle along by my side to the place of burial. And here, by the side of poor Butterworth, we had opened Bertie's newly-closed grave. To that grave I now consigned the dear mother, then laid her infant child upon her breast, and, with my double loss before me, read the remaining part of the service. At the words 'earth to earth' most of the Christians cast in a handful of the soil. Nellie and I now threw in our little bunches of flowers, and the native Christians followed our example. The grave was then filled up, and we then sung two hymns in Kinika. A literal translation of the first, which was composed by Mr. Rebmann, of Rabai, would be as follows:

'Above is our home:
　　Above, above it is.
Below we are strangers:
　　It is not our home.

But above, above,
　　How shall I reach?
He who shall raise me,
　　Who is it? who is it?

I will tell you,
　　Only listen;
Is it not Jesus Christ,
　　The only good Master?

He descended
　　Upon the earth,
And He loved men:
　　Have you not the news?

If you lay hold on Him
　　With a true faith,
You shall arrive above
　　To rejoice.　Amen.'

"We also sang a translation of the English hymn, 'Canaan, bright Canaan,' not only on account of the appropriateness of the sentiment, but also because I have regarded it as Mrs. Wakefield's hymn; for she importuned me so much that I was compelled to translate it for the people. It owes its existence in Kinika purely to her; and was the last hymn she taught the people to sing. She printed the whole of it in very large Roman characters, gummed it on to two boards, and hung it up in the verandah, where she gathered the people together, and taught it to them. This hymn, together with many others of her printing, still hangs there; and the boys, as they pass along, are often tempted to linger and sing it. They often sing it in their domicile, and on the Sabbath it rings well through the house of worship. Rendered back literally from Kinika into English it would be as follows :—

MRS. WAKEFIELD.   MR. BUTTERWORTH.   MR. NEW.

'Oh, how well has Jesus done,
   He came out of the land of Canaan;
And on the tree He surely died
   That I might go to Canaan.
A beautiful crown appears
   In the land of Canaan,
And a staff of victory,
   Come let us go to Canaan.
Canaan, oh Canaan, &c.

When I reach the congregation
   Yonder in the land of Canaan,
I will sing with them earnestly
   In the joys of Canaan.
Yonder Jesus sits
   On His throne in Canaan,
Calling His children
   That they may dwell with Him in Canaan.
Canaan, oh Canaan, &c.

Turn, heathen,
   Let us go together to Canaan.
Jesus waits, and angels,
   To welcome thee to Canaan,
Be washed from thy vileness,
   There is no evil in Canaan;
All the people are holy ones
   Who dwell in Canaan.
Canaan, oh Canaan, &c.'

"Mrs. Wakefield had been very anxious to add 'Canaan,' to the hymns we already possessed, as she thought that both the music and the words would be much liked by the boys. I told her that it was not a difficult matter merely to translate the hymn into Kinika; but that it *was* difficult to make a translation and, at the same time, to preserve the same number of feet as in the original. 'Oh,' she rejoined, 'you can put it in *this* way, and *that* way, and alter it thus, and thus,' and in this way the thing was accomplished. Immediately upon my handing her the manuscript, she went to the piano, played and sung it through, and at once commenced teaching it to the people. We little thought when this hymn was composed, how soon she would 'reach the congregation,' and sing with them 'in the joys of Canaan.' One knew, and only One.

"Besides the native Christians there were nearly fifty heathen Wanika standing round the grave, and at my request George David preached to them of 'Jesus and the Resurrection.'

"Nellie and I then, hand in hand, come back to our homeless and desolate house. May God bring us in His own good time to meet again with those from whom we are now severed, there to part no more."

SUPPLEMENTARY CHAPTER.

Natives' Letters.—Conclusion.

THE time immediately following Mrs. Wakefield's removal from this world, was one of great sorrow at the Mission at Ribé. That Mrs. Wakefield had been much beloved by the people among whom she had lived, and for whom she had, at last, laid down her life, will be evident from the letters the writer received from them shortly afterwards, translations of some of which are here presented to the reader. Many more might be given, but these must suffice.

(I.—From Dado.)

"Ribé, July 18th, 1873.

"Rev. and Dear Sir,—I am very sorry to tell you that your dear sister has gone home to her Saviour, together with her beloved son, who was born last month. The child died on Saturday morning, the 12th inst., and was buried in the afternoon by his father. And soon after the mother died also. We were very sorry to lose her who had been so kind to us; more than we expected from her. May God quiet your heart, that you may bear the loss with patience. And she was a very good lady to us, and she was very kind to all. She taught us to sing, and write, and read, and she taught us many things. We believe she is in heaven.—Dado."

(II.—From Kamnazo.)

"Ribé, July 18th, 1873.

"My Dear Sir,—I send you a letter which will pain your heart. Your sister gave birth to a healthy and strong son.

NATIVES' LETTERS—CONCLUSION.

He lived for a month and four days, and then died. Four days afterwards his mother died. Oh! and I am very sad! It was she herself who taught me the way of eternal life. If she had remained till now she would have taught me more. But now God has called her, and she has answered. And I wish to hold fast the words which she taught me. When I could not read it was she herself who taught me, and to write also. It was *she* who taught me *all*. And to sew she also taught me. And when I had an ulcer she herself applied the poultices to it. And if I had a torn jacket it was she who mended it for me. But now she dwells on high in heaven. She came with a torch here to the land of Ribé that all the people might take it, and each one be enlightened in his mind, and when the last day shall come be prepared for the Son of Man when he cometh.—It is I, KAMNAZO WA CHAI."

In January of the following year, a very gracious religious awakening occurred at Ribé, and the tidings of this are conveyed in the following letter from Kamnazo. He says:

"Ribé, January 14th, 1874.

"MY DEAR SIR AND FRIEND,—I write to you the news which are of Ribé. The tidings are these. On the first Sabbath of the New Year I saw very great things indeed! Your brother-in-law did that which I have never seen before since my birth. And that which my father nor mother ever saw, nor other Ribé people whatever. Your brother-in-law put a *penitents' form!* and there, at that spot, I found the joy! But for a long time before this I had been very wicked. I was told the words of the Gospel very many days, but I did not believe them. But on that day of the penitents' form I also was enabled to repent. And I hope that God will be with me for ever and ever. The peace of this my joy is the fruit of the words of which I am in the possession, and those words were told me by Mr. Wakefield.

"Well, then, and may God be with me. I pray to God for you: do you pray to God for me? And I trust that God is with me; and I hope, also, that when I die I shall die in the hands of Jesus. If we do not meet in this world we shall see each other above in heaven. May peace be with you and with the friends, with *all* of them.

"And about Helena. She is well. Helena is well, and I wish that God may be with her until she is old, that she may serve our Lord Jesus Christ. May she trust on until she dies, that she may die in the hands of Jesus. And I, when I am taking Helena out in the morning for her walk, I ask her where her mamma is? She says, 'Why, she has died.' I say, 'Yes, but *where is* she?' Helena says, 'Why, she is on high, and the baby too, and also Heri.' I say to her again, 'Well, do you want to follow your mamma?' She says, 'Yes, I do; also for all the boys to go, all of them.' 'Let us go,' she continues, 'and see mamma and baby and Heri.' I say to her again, 'Well, do you want to follow your mamma?' She says, 'Yes, I do! and also for all the boys to go, all of them.' 'Let us go,' she continues, 'and see mamma, and baby, and Heri,' and at the last she speaks joyfully.

"Oh my soul, thou hast been born in sin. From thy infancy thou hast been nursed in evil. Now, then, O my soul, *choose*, for there are but two masters. One is He who created thee, but the other is a *Thief!* Well, my soul, thou canst not stand still between these two. If you grasp hold of God in truth, and with a genuine heart, He will save you from the fire which is to come.

"And I, I wish the Ribé people to come to God that He may bless the whole of them.

It is I,

KAMNAZO,

who was wicked, but now Jesus blesses me.

"Good-bye, my dear Sir."

The case of Heri, referred to in the above letter, is a very interesting one, and as it stands connected with Mrs. Wakefield's work may suitably find a place here. Mr. Wakefield thus relates his history.

"Years ago, in the far interior of Africa, there lived a heathen man named Heri. He used often to go out into the forest to hunt buffaloes. One day he had succeeded in shooting one of these wild animals with an arrow, when the infuriated animal rushed upon him and tossed him high in the air with its horns. He fell to the ground with a very heavy fall, and was much hurt. Heri, however, still fought the buffalo, and at length killed him. He never, however, overgot the effects of his fall, and it brought on a disease which many years afterwards ended in his death. One day when Heri was travelling as a porter towards the sea coast, he was sold into slavery by some of his fellow-countrymen, and taken across the sea to Arabia. At length he obtained his freedom and came to Mombas. About nine years ago he built himself a hut, about three miles from our Ribé Mission Station. He was then about fifty years of age.

"Early one Sabbath morning last summer Mgomba went out to the villages to invite the people to come to the preaching. He came back with a smiling face, and said that among many others, Heri had promised to come. Heri came, and when I put out my hand and bade him welcome, he said, with a smile, 'Yes, I'm come,' as though *he* was very glad he had come too. Mrs. Wakefield and I talked with him, and tried to do him good. Little did my dear wife think at that time how soon both herself and Heri would be in heaven. Heri went into the Sabbath-school that day, and also attended the preaching service, and from that time he came regularly. The last time he came was during Mrs. Wakefield's illness, on that sad Sunday morning when we were both weeping over the loss of our dear Bertie; and old Heri tried to comfort us in our sorrow.

"About three weeks after Mrs. Wakefield's death a message came to me from Heri to say that he was very ill, and wished me very much to go to see him. I went, taking

Nellie with me, and found him very weak. He said to me, 'I am very ill, and whether I shall die or not I do not know; but I have sent for my missionary to tell you that I do not wish to die a heathen, but I want to die a Christian. I wish,' he continued, 'not to be buried by the heathen Wanika according to their customs; but I wish to be buried at the mission, amongst the people of the Book.'

"I had a great deal of talk with this poor old man, and found him thoroughly determined to be a Christian altogether. When I saw some heathenish charms tied round his neck and told him they must be given up, he immediately complied, and before a knife could be found to cut the string, had broken it with his hands and scattered the things across the floor. After a long talk with him I baptized him. The next morning, just after sunrise, Heri died. His last words were, 'O Lord, cleanse me from sin; take all evil out of my heart; give me a good heart, for the sake of Jesus Christ. Amen.'

"He was, as he had requested, buried in our little mission burying-place, not far from Mrs. Wakefield's grave. My dear wife had assisted me in leading Heri to the Saviour, and perhaps she was the first to meet him at the gates of heaven and bid him welcome."

As Mr. Wakefield was now left quite alone, his care of his little daughter (whose health was often in a very delicate state,) in addition to the responsibilities of the mission, weighed heavily upon him. Sometimes, for her greater safety, he took Nellie with him on his missionary journeys. Here is one such incident.

"The heathen people of Duruma have of late become very anxious to have a mission established among them. I paid them one visit before my dear wife's illness, and intended to go again as soon as she should recover, and take her with me. As soon as I could make it convenient after her death, I set off upon this journey, accompanied only by Nellie and some of the mission people. The heavy showers which fell in the morning delayed our starting till noon. Then, with Nellie seated in her little chair on the donkey's back, myself walking by her side, and the porters following, we set off through the long grass of the jungle, and over hill and dale, on our way to Duruma. After we had travelled about nine miles we reached Rabai, where the Church of England has a Mission Station. Here we rested for an hour, as we were both tired and hungry. The black people who were in charge of the mission were very kind to us, and gave Nellie a nice dinner of rice and curry, and we proceeded on our journey.

"As we neared Duruma, Mgomba, who was then carrying Nellie in his arms, stopped all at once as if he had heard some dreadful sound, and cried out, 'What's that?' He heard a shrill whistle in the jungle behind us, and he was afraid the terrible Masai warriors were coming upon us. After waiting a time we found, however, that it was only one of our own party who had whistled, so we went on again.

"At length we reached Duruma, where we received a very kind welcome. After getting our supper we prepared for rest. Our hut was of a good large size, but had no windows in it, no fireplace or chimney, and the door was only a yard high, so I had to stoop very much to get in at all. There was a fire in the middle of the hut, so the place was very smoky. Seven other people came into the hut to sleep, besides Nellie and me, and besides these, there were twenty or thirty goats and sheep, which kept up quite a concert of noise the whole night long. The bedstead on which Nellie and I slept was a lot of sticks laid across three or four pieces of wood. It amused me to see the man 'making my bed,' which he did by rubbing his hand backwards and forwards over the sticks till they were all tolerably even. I laid my rug and my blankets on these sticks, and then we lay down and tried to sleep.

"The next day the people were called together that I

might preach to them, and that they might tell me if they wished to become Christians. The largest congregation I have ever preached to in East Africa assembled together. At first I spoke to Mgomba, and he interpreted what I said to the people. Soon, however, they told Mgomba he might stand aside. They said, ' No, no, we don't want *you* or any-one else to interpret; we thoroughly understand all the white man says, and we will talk with him ourselves.' After the preliminaries were over I sprang to my feet, and with Mrs. Wakefield's Bible in my hand I preached to them for nearly an hour. I thought, as God's Providence had prevented my dear wife herself from coming, that her Bible should come; and from it I preached Jesus to them. They listened to the sermon with great attention. It was the first time in their lives they had heard the wonderful story of God's love to them, and it gave me great joy to tell them of it.

"When the sermon was over the people all went aside to talk the matter over among themselves, and give me their reply. At length all was ready, and they came back. I stood up, anxious to receive their answer. It was given in the African fashion. An old man came and stood up close to me, and began to converse loudly with another man, every now and then appealing to the people to ask if they did not approve what he was saying. The people answered by loud applause. The reply was not only favourable—it was enthusiastic. The old man said, 'We all wish you to come and establish a mission among us. The country is yours. White man, you are our father. You are *my father*,' cried the old man, who, I should judge, was seventy years of age. I told them how pleased I was with their answer; that I loved them tenderly and deeply; but that my Master had said, 'If they do not receive you in one city, go to another.' As they had received me I would do my best to bring and send them the Gospel, and would soon come back to them again to fix on a spot for building a better hut to live in during my visits.

NATIVES' LETTERS—CONCLUSION.

"After I had bid the people good-bye, the young men, for my honour and amusement, formed a circle and gave the 'War Dance,' singing and shouting by way of accompaniment. They then rushed on farther, and came and danced again, and so on many times. Nellie looked on with astonishment and wondered what it all meant.

"The next day we returned safely to Ribé."

Even at Ribé Nellie's experiences were sometimes of an exciting character. Mr. Wakefield says:

"Very early one morning, long before it was light, I awoke to find that our bedroom was being invaded by swarms of black ants, which attack ferociously and bite severely. They were marching all over the floor in black masses, and here and there were climbing up the various articles of furniture in search of food. To have stepped out on to the floor would have been to have been dreadfully stung and bitten by these nasty little savages. I was very poorly too, and Nellie, who had been very restless all the night, was now asleep. The bell rang for prayers about half past five o'clock; but I felt too unwell to go, and besides I could not leave Nellie under these circumstances. So I sent a message that the people were to conduct prayers without me, and that afterwards one of the boys should come into my room with a firebrand to destroy and drive away the ants. Weary and poorly, I then fell asleep, and after a time the boy came in and began dashing the fire about, right and left, upon the floor, without waking me. Suddenly, however, I heard the loud cry, 'Master! master!' and on looking up saw that the muslin bed-curtains were all in a blaze. I seized Nellie, who was lying asleep by my side, lifted her over the bed, set her on her feet on the floor, and told her to trot away as fast as ever she could, which she did. I then seized one of the pillows, and smote the flames in every direction. As this did not put the fire out, I then tore down the curtains, and at last succeeded in stopping the spread of the flames. We were very thankful that things were no worse, for if the fire could not have been stopped, Nellie and I should have seen our house burnt to the ground."

On another occasion Mr. Wakefield took Nellie with him to Duruma, going by way of Mombas, and here, as everywhere, was touched by the kind interest that was manifested by the people in his little motherless child. He says:

"On my third visit to Duruma I went by way of Mombas, taking Nellie and some of the boys with me. I have been quite affected by the sympathy which the people of Mombas have shown with me in my great sorrow, and especially by their kindness to my motherless little child. One afternoon Nellie asked me if Tofiki might go with her to our old house to roast some green Indian corn, which some one had given her, and of which she is very fond. When they came back, Tofiki said: 'Oh! the Sawahili women do feel very much for Nellie. Some of them said, "Poor child, she has no mother now! I wish I could have her to take care of, and to nurse."' I felt the tears coming to my eyes when Tofiki told me this. An old Hindoo, a greyheaded man, was quite excited as Nellie and I passed his little shop. He ran out after her, as he had seen her before, but Nellie was shy, as she had forgotten him. 'Well,' he said, 'I'll bring you something to-night.' And though he was a poor Hindoo washerman, he came as he said, and inquired, 'Where's the little Miss? I *said* I would come.' But Nellie was asleep. He then uncovered a large dish of Indian sweetmeats (cakes) which his wife had made. 'Oh!' he said, 'she was my little girl's friend.' They used to play together. Nellie had also a plate of fruit given her at the house of another Hindoo. Every day during our stay at Mombas a slave came in with a covered plate of nice things, and called out, 'Helena! this is for you.' The children and slave-girls often assembled under our windows, shouting up, 'Helena, come!' Her name is known in Mombas far and wide."

Here is a pleasant reminiscence of Mrs. Wakefield's life at Mombas, furnished by her husband,

"It is Saturday night while I am writing. This afternoon Nellie and I took a walk for about two miles along the seashore. All the way I could not help thinking of former times. The walk is a beautiful one, and Mrs. Wakefield and Nellie and I have been along it many a time together. But there was one wanting to-day. I gathered some pretty flowers for Nellie. Mrs. Wakefield and I have gathered the same kind on the same walk many a time; but now she has found more beautiful flowers in Paradise.

"I remember a walk that Mrs. Wakefield and I took together at Zanzibar soon after our arrival in Africa, and as I do not think she has ever told you about it I will do so now.

"We left our house about half-past four in the afternoon, and returned at sunset, and a more delightful ramble we could scarcely have had. Mrs. Wakefield said it reminded her very much of a walk through the meadows of her own beloved Mountsorrel in England, the grassy path was so soft and the rich verdure so abundant all around. Crossing over a grassy plain, called by the Zanzibar people Waza-Moya, we entered a narrow green lane, bounded on each side by a high bushy hedge, the foliage of which was of a more rich and delicate green that we see in England. Beyond the hedges were plantations. Mrs. Wakefield gathered some pretty wild flowers, some of them were much like the English sweet pea, and were both white and coloured. Others were convolvulus-shaped, some yellow and some blue. We soon found ourselves passing through a grove of orange trees, all laden with fruit, and bending low over the pathway. Only one orange here and there had a tinge of yellow, the rest were of a rich dark green; but even in this state they look luxuriant, and Mrs Wakefield stood looking round her with delight. There were lemon trees and limes, too, and far above these the 'feathery palm trees' raised their heads, the graceful fronds waving gently in the breeze, while young cocoa-nuts clustered thickly underneath their cool shade. The owners of these orange-groves are very kind, and have often given me permission to wander among the trees and pluck and eat as I like, but on this occasion we saw no one about, so we looked and passed on.

"Before reaching home we passed a Hindoo cemetery full of white stone tombs, with long grass growing between. We also met numbers of native men and women, wearing long white 'night-dresses,' and carrying baskets of fruit, singing as they went along. My wife was much amused at the fantastic way in which many of the girls arrange their hair, which is short and curly. They divide it into horizontal stripes from front to back by partings an inch or so from each other, and make one long curl of the hair between, running right over the head.

"One sight, however, made us feel sad, and somewhat spoiled our pleasant walk. Here and there human bones, and in some places almost entire skeletons, lay across our pathway. The cholera had swept away many thousand of persons from Zanzibar only a short time before until there was no place to bury, and many of the dead were merely carried outside the city, and thrown away among the bushes, to be devoured by wild dogs and birds of prey.

"We reached home from our walk just as the sun was going down."

At length, a year and two months after her mother's death, Nellie was committed to the kind care of Mr. and Mrs. Chancellor, of the Church of England Society, for conveyance to England, in the hope that her health, which was fast failing might be restored and her life spared. She was now nearly four years old, could converse freely in native African, but understood all that was said to her in English, though beyond a few short words she did not speak it. The parting of her father from his child was a very trying one to himself. A glance at his letter of that time will give us some idea of his feelings in prospect of the separation. He writes:

"Mombas, September the 7th, 1874.—This is Monday morning, and the time is seven o'clock. I spent yesterday and the day before on board the *Sultana* with Nellie and the Chancellors. I am now wondering what sort of a night they have had with Nellie, and how my little pet looks this morning, now she finds that papa is not on board. I sent Tofiki a short time ago to the ship to fetch some things I had left behind, and to take a few of Nellie's things which had been left in the house. Ah, here comes Tofiki back again! Nellie has passed a good night. On Saturday night we began the process of preparing Nellie for separation from me. She slept with the Chancellors in the cabin while I slept on deck. She cried in the night and called 'papa,' but of course I didn't speak.

"After I had put her to bed last night on board the *Sultana*, I stole a kiss from her, which was my 'good-bye, darling,' should I not see her again before she leaves. May God, the everlasting Father, take loving care of our little orphan! May He enclose all the passengers in His everlasting arms, and lead them safely to their destination."

"Monday evening.—I have been watching Nellie nearly all the afternoon from our house, through a good telescope, and have been delighted beyond measure at the way in which she has been bearing up under her trying circumstances. She has been going to and fro about the deck with Mrs. Chancellor and Dado, and evidently behaving herself well. When sometimes they saw me, Mr. or Mrs. Chancellor would lift Nellie up and point me out to her, and get her to wave her pocket-handkerchief. I also waved mine, and we held quite a conversation together."

"Monday night.—It is now 11 p.m., and I have just been on a visit to the ship to take a farewell look at my little pet. My plan was to go and give her a kiss in her sleep, and quietly come away. But she heard my name mentioned, then heard my voice, and woke up completely. I nursed her for some time, and she put her arms lovingly around my neck, and we had a little chat. I then got her to sleep, put her to bed, and then, very reluctantly, left her." The next morning, about seven o'clock, the vessel steamed out of the harbour and took the little passenger far, far away.

Nellie reached England safely on Monday morning, October 27th, 1874. And after nearly five years more had passed it was her pleasure to meet her dear papa once more. It was on Saturday afternoon, March 29th, 1879, when Mr. Wakefield arrived at 153, Rock Street, Sheffield, from Southampton. Nellie had been watching at the window for her papa for a long time, but just at that moment had been called away. Her papa's loud "Rat tat" at the door, however, soon recalled her, and when the door was flung open, and the father and child met once more, the sight was one not soon to be forgotten.

Little more now remains to be told. During the last decade several changes and many improvements have taken place in connection with this East African Mission. The work at Ribé is in a prosperous condition. The Rev. T. H. Carthew, the superintendent of the Mission, says, writing at the close of 1887:

"On Tuesday we left for Ribé to induct Mr. Heroe into office, it having been decided that he should take charge of that station.

"The road to Ribé, if indeed it may be called a road, is a very zigzag one, running up and down, in and out, now lost in tall grass, now in bush, then by a strip of cultivated land, then on open plain; in fact, a variety unique in its character, beautiful, rugged, and sublime. We were received with great rejoicing. Ribé is a pretty place. The prospect from the Mission-house is charming. It is about 500 feet higher than Jomvu, and this fact alone would indicate that it must be a healthier place to live at. On our arrival there a delightful breeze was blowing from the sea, which could be seen in the distance across an outstretch of country and picturesque scenery which to me looked magnificent.

"On the Wednesday morning we conducted service in our little church. We had 200 people present, and Mr. Heroe was well received by them. Immediately after service we went to the graves of the Missionaries who received the Master's call, "Come up hither," from the Mission field— Edmund Butterworth, Charles New, John Martin, and Mrs. Wakefield. I was much impressed while I stood there gazing on the monuments of the dead. It was well to look, but not to linger. I came away, if a sadder, yet I trust a better and a stronger man. The Lord help me to act well my part. 'There all the honour lies.' After breakfast I received deputations from different tribes who had come to offer me their congratulations. I was pleased with the position and prospects of our Ribé station. A great work has been done there."

Mr. Carthew also visited the outstations in the Duruma country which are under the care of John ·Mgomba and Mazera respectively. He says:

"The Tuesday following our visit to Ribé, Mr. During and I visted Duruma. This place is about the same distance as Ribé from Jomvu; the road thither, however, is much clearer of bush and grass than the road to Ribé. There are hundreds of acres of land, which present an appearance similar to that of an English orchard very thinly planted with trees. The antics of my donkey on an open plain would not admit of close observation; in a narrow pathway, with grass or bush on either side, I could hold the brute in check, but in open field I was more than checkmated. My impression as I went along was this: that the district offered a most inviting and promising field for agriculture, and if by any means the land could only be worked, it would yield a harvest in rich abundance. We received a very hearty welcome at Duruma. The people, in a most genuine manner, expressed their pleasure at our arrival. As we approached the village they came to meet us in dance and song. My donkey seemed to catch something of the inspiration of the moment. Whether he felt the dignity of his calling, or thought it proper and right to join in the outburst of joy, or whether it was his mocking sarcasm, or his bliss in prospect of being relieved of fifteen stone, I cannot say; but, whatever might have been the moving or motive power, he roared out such a bray that nearly lifted me from his back in a fit of laughter. The village is situated on the immediate highway to the interior. The proposed railway from Mombas to the lake district is intended to pass close by, if not through the station. This will give us a vantage-ground and prominence of considerable value. We remained over night, and conducted service in the morning, at which about 200 were present.

"Duruma is a younger Mission-station than Jomvu, but there is every element present to make it a much stronger and more hopeful place. It requires immediately the oversight of a European minister. I would gladly go and labour amongst the people there, and leave the superintendence of the Mission in better hands. I was exceedingly pleased with the position and prospects of Duruma station."

From the foregoing it will be seen that the headquarters of the Mission have been removed from Ribé to Jomvu, which is pleasantly situated on a creek having direct communication with Mombas. At Jomvu we have a flourishing station. Many of the Christian converts here have formerly been slaves, and are now rejoicing in a double liberty.

The Galla Mission has been successfully established at Golbanti, on the banks of the Tana river, about thirty miles from the sea. It has had, however, a chequered history. On Monday May 3rd, 1886, a horde of cruel Masai warriors swept down upon the station and massacred many of the native Christians and also, sad to say, the newly arrived Missionaries, the Rev. John and Mrs. Houghton, a sketch of whose Missionary career has since been published.*

---

* The Martyrs of Golbanti. By Robert Brewin. London, A. Crombie.

The Rev. W. H. During, a coloured minister from Sierra Leone, is at present residing at that station.

The Rev. Thomas Wakefield, after a residence of nearly three years in England, again married, and, in the early part of 1882, returned to East Africa, where he remained five years. He is once more in this country; and at their Annual Assembly of 1888 the United Methodist Free Churches elected him as the President of the denomination, an honour to which his distinguished abilities and long and faithful service on the Mission field of Eastern Africa have richly entitled him. Nellie still lives; and, following her mother's footsteps, takes a lively interest in the spread of the Gospel in heathen lands.

The End.